Ulya Vogt-Göknil
Henri Stierlin (Ed.)

Ottoman Turkey

Photos: Eduard Widmer
Preface: Jürgen Joedicke

Benedikt Taschen

Editor of series   Henri Stierlin
Plans   Georges Berthoud EPF SIA

Editor of English edition   Kenneth Martin Leake

Contents

Preface

by Jürgen Joedicke

The invitation to write a preface to this book on Turkish architecture gives me the opportunity to thank that country and its wonderful people, whose hospitality I was able to enjoy during my two visits as a guest professor at the Technical University, Istanbul. All the things I have experienced – especially during my second visit, when experience was based on the first and was more systematically arranged – were not considered from the standpoint of an historian looking at historical monuments, but through the eyes of an architect, discovering in the mirror of the past certain problems of his own time (though not without any influence of architectural devotions of long standing). When considering Turkish mosques I have come to the conclusion that the problems of building do not vary so much in each epoch; what has changed are the means to solve them and the general social background.

I would like to advise anybody who visits Turkey via Istanbul to travel by ship and not by air or rail. As the ship sails into the Bosporus, past the Sultan Ahmet Cami, the Hagia Sophia and the Top-Kapi Palace (Sultan's Palace), the visitor will confirm what Le Corbusier (then aged twenty-five) had experienced in 1911 and had found so important as to reiterate it in his autobiography: 'The walls of Byzanz, the mosque of Sultan Ahmet, the Hagia Sophia, the great Top-Kapi Palace. For you, my dear townspeople, on the map : silhouettes !'

Ulya Vogt-Göknil has mentioned in her text certain principles of Turkish town-planning, among which I find the emphasis on topography very important. The Turkish town nestles against the formation of the countryside and reaches its dominating point where the countryside also reaches its most extreme point. Accordingly, Sultans' mosques are not to be found in the center of the city or as a 'point de vue' of representative cross-roads, but instead at the summits of the surrounding hills. If one were to abandon technical descriptions and simply steep oneself in the magic of Istanbul, then, perhaps, one could say that, with their silhouette of cascade-like descending domes, the mosques seem to be a formation of nature emphasized by architectural means. This statement seems the more surprising if one remembers that a mosque consists of elementary geometrical forms – ashlar (sometimes cube), sphere or cylinder. They are the same geometrical forms which Le Corbusier proclaimed as fundamentals in his aesthetics ; in fact he called them the 'beautiful forms' and 'the language of humanity'.

I found the following sentence in one of the popular descriptions of Turkey's sights : 'It is not worth visiting more than one mosque, because they are basically all alike.' This sentence reveals a lack of understanding and can only be found in popular travel books. The historical development of Ottoman mosques is still one of the cinderellas of the history of architecture. Yet it is one of the most fascinating examples of the beginning of an architecture rendered finite through space, an architecture which obtains complete identity of space and visual exterior form. Its renunciation of pictorial exhibition (be it plastic or artistic) leads to a

reduction of all architectural elements to those that are exclusively space-defined. It also identifies the floor – concerned with seating facilities in the cathedrals and churches of Europe – as a space-defined area.

The typology of space evolves from the quadratic room covered with one dome, and the two-domed mosque with adjoining aisles, to more and more variations of hemispherical domes surrounding the main dome with adjoining aisles,

also dome-covered. Within these externally visual forms the interior always accomplishes new solutions and differentiations in primary and secondary rooms and also partly in primary, secondary and tertiary rooms.

One is continually surprised by the simple means which are employed for room structure. Near the car-ferry quay in Usküdar lies the Semsi Ahmet Pasha Cami, built by Sinan in 1580, a small site consisting of mosque and medrese. The L-shaped medrese is not constructed parallel to the narrow side and alongside the mosque, but at an acute angle. Thus

between the mosque and medrese a space is created, bordered by simple means but highly differentiated, whose effect is heightened by its skilful positioning in the topography. While the entrance is situated inland at the most narrow part between mosque and medrese, one discovers, after having passed the narrow and longer side of the mosque, a space between the mosque and medrese, which extends far over the hills surrounded by the water of the Bosporus.

Among the many problems and questions which arise from a study of Ottoman mosques, I would like to mention finally the question of the construction of these airy domed buildings. We cannot trace any definite documentary references that would, for example, allow a static investigation. Even in reconstructions the dome form is based in most cases on assumptions. The

5

general belief that the domes are actually 'skull-caps' has, so far, not been proved by exact measurements. Moreover, details on the development of the vaults are not readily available.

My own investigations on the Mihrimah Cami have proved that it has no rib-vaulting, as was used by the Romans, neither a construction of joined earthenware pipes, like the dome building of Ravenna, but a construction based on flat tiles running radial to the dome's center and tangential to the dome's curvature, the latter being embedded within a more or less equally thick layer of chalk plaster. The steep vaults are diverted over the pendentives on to the four main pillars. Since these pillars reach far to the top, while the point of the resultant lies very far below at the beginning of the 'Gurtbogen,' there is sufficient vertical stress to press the resultant inwards and to transmit it through the pillars to the base.

This transmission of stress confirms a realization which meanwhile has been made in the Hagia Sophia: namely, that even with the arrangement of half-domes the bulk of the weight is carried by the four main pillars. An investigation carried out on the Hagia Sophia showed that the predominant part of the weight of the vaults is taken up by the four main pillars and only a small portion by the axis situated in the half-domes. If these half-domes, as is generally believed, are really necessary for the stability of extended domes, then all those buildings in which the edge of the dome is not secured on all sides, would be inexplicable.

These mosques and their domes dominated the panorama of the cities and were in many ways connected with city life. Perhaps it would be easiest to explain their significance by comparing them with a civic center. The mosque, a place of worship which is visited several times during the day for quiet prayer, was built conjointly with a school, a hospital, an alms-kitchen, a pharmacy and an inn (caravanserai). Shops and cafés, the men's meeting place, also formed part of this huge site.

The town center was another construction, of

busy passages and quiet blind-alleys, around which anything from five to ten houses formed an independent locality. Kemal Ahmet Aru, Professor of Town-planning at the Technical University, Istanbul, has said 'the blind alley is a private meeting place for its inhabitants. It is here we find the sociological living structure of Turkish towns.' This remark is distinguished by its integration as opposed to segregation, since poor and rich lived together.

Since wealth was always regarded as a possible danger to the strict ideal of orthodox godliness – a spring of temptation – it was only sanctioned if the wealthy man identified his purpose as a donor and shared his wealth with the poor. Thus the number of public buildings such as schools, caravanserais and baths, as well as the beautifully designed fountains, increased continuously. Together with the mosques they dominated the appearance of the old Turkish town and, with their style, building material and site, struck the largest imaginable contrast to the houses which consisted generally of wood. This can be seen partly in present-day Istanbul or in the older parts of Ankara situated on the Burgberg. We only hope that the many efforts to preserve and restore parts of such dwellings will be crowned with success.

Ulya Vogt-Göknil has described the equipment and site of these houses in detail, so that any further remarks would be mere repetition. But I would like to mention the formal structure of the wall, which is parted into posts and, from post to post, into a row of windows – an arrangement mainly customary in summer residences on the Bosporus.

The meaning of this great and individual architecture disappeared with the acceptance of new European ideas in the nineteenth century. But, unfortunately, the architectural style imported from Europe during that time was

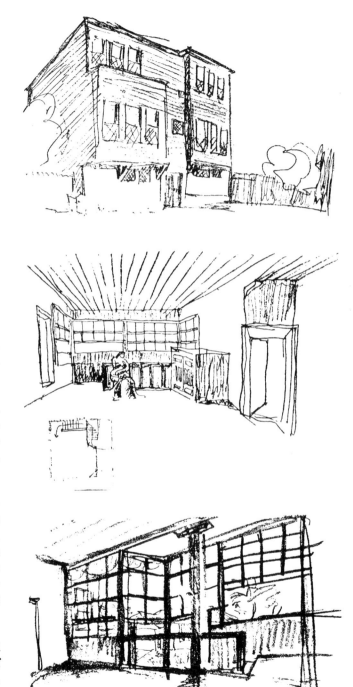

without quality. Therefore, we may find in Istanbul anachronisms like neo-gothic mosques or Renaissance monstrosities like the Dolmabahce Palace.

The renewal of the Turkish State under Atatürk led to a new and terrible clash between Turkish and European thought. In Ankara, the Anatolian city which Atatürk made the capital, Bonatz, Egli, Elsaesser and Holzmeister had built in their traditional way, thus defining the character of the city. But we also find in Ankara the last building by Bruno Taut, the protagonist of the modern, who lectured during the last years of his life in Istanbul. His successor should have been Polzig who died, however, shortly before moving to Istanbul.

First modern architectural attempts can be found during the 'thirties. During World War II and thereafter, Turkish architecture tended towards the conservative. Around 1950 stronger modern tendencies became apparent. As in every country, Turkish architecture has to prove her existence in this modern world – not only the achievements of means and needs, but also, possibly through her buildings, the creation of a new Turkish society.

Stuttgart, July 1965

The illustrations in the preface are from Le Corbusier's 'Carnets de Voyage'

The Origins and Development of the Ottoman Empire

Asia Minor before the foundation of the Ottoman Empire

In the light of recent archaeological discoveries, the history of the peninsula of Asia Minor on which the Ottoman Turks established their Empire at the end of the fourteenth century can now be traced back to the twentieth century B.C. The first people to settle in Asia Minor and establish an empire were the Hittites and the last were the Turks. During that time, Asia Minor remained a link between Asia and Europe, the setting for mass invasions and wars which were to affect the course of world history. The Anatolian plateau, a mountain range stretching from the Black Sea to the Mediterranean, formed an ideal bridge between the two continents.

The invasion of the Phrygians at the end of the thirteenth century B.C. marked the end of the Hittite Empire. The new Phrygian Empire, however, was itself short-lived. Medes and Persians from the East, Lydians and Greeks from the West, began to settle on the peninsula. At the turn of the sixth century B.C. Persian armies campaigned through Asia Minor towards Greece. A century later, about 336 B.C., another powerful force made itself felt in the opposite quarter: the armies of Alexander the Great marched through the peninsula to invade central Asia. After the Roman Empire had been divided, Asia Minor was no longer a colony; under Roman rule she became part of the new Byzantine Empire. During the first part of the eleventh century A.D. Turkish tribes began immigrating from the East.

The first clash between the Seljuk Turks and the Byzantines occurred as early as 1071. Byzantine troops penetrated far eastwards to check the Turkish advance. At the battle of Malazgirt (north of Lake Van) the Turks, however, defeated the Byzantines and continued westwards.

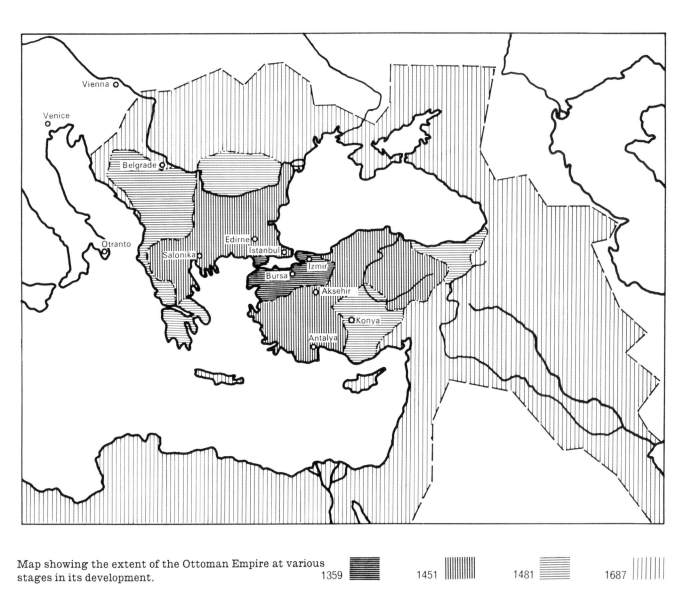

Map showing the extent of the Ottoman Empire at various stages in its development.

1359 ▬ 1451 ▓ 1481 ▤ 1687 ▥

Ten years after the victory of Malazgirt, the Turks had almost reached Constantinople. Having captured the town of Nikea (Iznik) they made it their capital.

In 1092 Kilic-Arslan assumed independent control of the Turkish tribes now established in Asia Minor. In order to distinguish themselves from the Great Seljuk Empire in the East the Seljuks in Asia Minor called the new Sultanate the Seljuks of Rum (rum : west). In 1097 the First Crusade provided the Byzantines with a fresh excuse to attack. Joining the crusaders, they advanced on the Seljuks, recapturing Nikea and driving Kilic-Arslan's army to retreat to the hinterland. It was about this time that Konya was made capital of the West Seljuk Empire. However, Byzantine loyalties changed with the Second Crusade; faced with this common enemy, they came to a valuable understanding with their Seljuk opponents. The Seljuks succeeded in halting the Second Crusade near Eskisehir about 1150, and caused its subsequent failure. Fifty years later, however, the Third Crusade, led by Frederick Barbarossa, progressed with the consent of the Seljuks, who offered full protection. The Seljuk empire had been firmly established and was accepted in the west, whereas Byzantine power was on the wane. The Fourth Crusade stormed Constantinople, marking the end of the Byzantine empire, and thus enabled the Seljuks to extend their frontiers from the Mediterranean to the Black Sea. At the beginning of the thirteenth century, Konya, the capital, became a religious and intellectual center. Architecture and, in particular, poetry flourished at this time; the Sultan's palace in Konya became a home for artists and mystics. The flourishing Seljuk Empire was now threatened from the East. The first attack on Asia Minor came in 1242 from the westward moving Mongols. This invasion marked the beginning of the Seljuk decline.

The Period before the Mongolian Invasion

By the end of the twelfth century, the West Seljuk Empire had disintegrated before the Mongolian challenge. Principalities and petty kingdoms of Nomadic origin now broke away from the Seljuks. Threatened by the Mongols, they had come to Asia Minor to seek protection in the Seljuk Empire, where they were welcomed as able warriors and given land in the frontier regions. They became frontier guards, and in this capacity their special duty was to protect the country's north-west territory from the feared western enemy, the Byzantines. After the Seljuk defeat, a desperate struggle broke out between these frontier kingdoms. In the Eastern region of Konya, the Karamanli assumed power. In the West, the sons of Osman devastated their neighbors before advancing on Byzantium. There were two reasons for the success of the Ottomans. The Mongolians' capacity for organization did not match their skill in war. Their sudden early successes had intoxicated them, undermining their strength and destroying their discipline. Soon they withdrew eastwards and abandoned the plundered Seljuk Empire. The second reason was the deterioration of the Byzantine Empire. After a thousand years, the Empire was now struggling to preserve itself, thus rendering any attack on the ravaged Seljukian territory out of the question.

This territory was to prove fateful for Osman's descendants. The Ottomans had already subdued their Turkish neighbors; in order to expand economically and find access to the sea, they had to challenge the Byzantines. Soon the Byzantine towns of Bursa and Nikea fell to them. Orhan, son of Osman, moved with his retinue to Bursa where he erected the first mosque. From 1326-1368, Bursa was the seat of the Ottomans. This period saw the construction of a great number of mosques, medreses, mausoleums, tombs and baths. Orhan's successors encouraged the master-builders to develop their talents, producing new ideas and forms which, from the outset, were fundamentally different from Seljukian as well as Byzantine styles.

By the middle of the fourteenth century, most of Asia Minor was occupied by the Ottomans, with the exception of Karamania and Kastamona on the Black Sea, which belonged to the Isfediyaroghi tribes. The first sortie into Europe had occurred during the reign of Orhan. This was followed up by several attacks on the Greek mainland and islands. In 1357 Gallipoli was captured, thus establishing the Ottoman's first European stronghold.

At the beginning of the fourteenth century, during the reign of Beyazid I, the Ottoman campaigns extended beyond Southern Greece to Hungary. This rapid advance was halted by the Mongolian ruler, Timur-Lenk, whose troops advanced as far as Ankara, capturing Beyazid after fierce fighting, then plundering Izmir (Smyrna) and Bursa. Beyazid died in prison and his empire disintegrated. His four sons all claimed succession; and apart from fighting each other they had also to face the Mongols and the minor kingdoms who now saw their chance to regain independence; but neither of the latter struggles was as fierce as the fight for succession. This lasted about ten years, by which time only two rivals were left : Mohamed I, who used his military strength to reunite the western part of Asia Minor ; and his brother Musâ, the ruler of Rumeh, which comprised the western territories. The tragic struggle between the two brothers ended in Musâ's death. Mohamed was then proclaimed absolute ruler.

Again the Mongols had been unable to follow up their advantage. Arnold Toynbee, writing on the behavior of the Ottomans at this time, regards the Mongolian attack as essentially a movement of provocation : 'What was the effect on the fortunes of the Ottomans when Timur Lenk (Tamerlane) took Beyazid Yilderim (the Sultan Beyazid) captive on the field of Ankara? This catastrophe overtook the Ottomans just when they were on the point of completing their conquest of the main body of Orthodox Christendom in the Balkan Peninsula. It was at this critical moment that they were prostrated, on the Asiatic side of the Straits, by a thunderbolt from Transoxania. A general collapse of their uncompleted edifice of empire is what might have been expected. But it was not what happened in fact; and half a century later, Mehmet the Conqueror

was able to place the coping-stone on Beyazid's building by taking possession of Constantinople.'

This Mongol defeat, however, had positive results. Where victory might have made them complacent, a setback strengthened their resistance.

Before The Conquest of Constantinople

In 1421 Murad II ascended the throne in the new capital of Edirne. His father, Mohamed I, had reunited the empire. His son, Mohamed II, was to capture the Byzantine capital of Constantinople thirty years later, thus establishing the final boundaries of the Empire. Murad's aims were to reorganize the army and his administration, rather than to wage war on neighboring territories. One of his most important undertakings was reorganizing the feudal system. He divided the country into large and small fiefs. In the event of war, the feudal Lords were bound by law to provide the State with cavalry, infantry and naval troops. A second, very daring, innovation which proved itself in subsequent generations, was the founding of the Yeni-Ceri, the Janissarian army, and its attendant schools. The army consisted of carefully selected children from the Christian minority, who were converted to Islam and sent to live with Turkish families. Once they had adapted themselves to the Turkish way of life and had served at least three years' apprenticeship, they were transferred to the Court where they were trained as soldiers in special military academies. Possibilities of advancement were unlimited for recruits from these academies – many Ottoman Viziers had been former pupils of the Janissarian schools. The Ottoman rulers thus made it possible for the Christian minority to play a part as regents in the government of the country.

By the beginning of the fifteenth century the

Turks were already a minority in their own Empire. Moreover, people in the countries which they had conquered were allowed to follow their own religious beliefs. There is no record of any attempts at mass conversion or religious persecution. Neither Byzantine nor Western historians (who delighted in accounts of Turkish atrocities) have touched on this. The Ottomans wanted to remain the dominant race and from the start they had refused to merge with their defeated enemies into a new racial unity. They did, however, compel Christian minorities to submit to the Rerschirme system of selection of boys : the sacrifice of this small but gifted élite was the price Christians had to pay for the freedom to pursue their own way of life. For the Turks, leadership meant keeping one's distance, yet preventing this from becoming an irreconcilable gap between victor and vanquished. The Rerschirme system created the necessary slender bridge between the Turkish rulers and their alien subjects. Toynbee considers this solution as a reason for the unusually long survival of the Ottoman State. The rapid but lasting successes of the Ottomans stand out, particularly by comparison with the short-lived victories of other Nomadic races. The Ottomans ruled various races and countries for four centuries. The Avars had swept over the Slavs, the Huns over Central Europe, the Mongols over Asia Minor, but none of these could hold sway for more than a lifetime. That the relatively small Ottoman minority was able to maintain its leadership for so long was due to the amount of reflection and calculation out of which their form of government had evolved. As Toynbee has noted, their greatest wisdom lay in the establishment of the Rerschirme system which by making use of an élite drawn from a particular group, enabled the outnumbered Turks to rule the mass of the populace.

The Conquest of Constantinople

When Mohamed II succeeded in 1451, war broke out again with Byzantium. His great grandfather, Beyazid, had built a fortress on the Anatolian side of the Bosporus at the narrowest point of the straits. By building a new fortress on the opposite side, Mohamed had now isolated the town of Constantinople completely. Ever since his accession, he had pursued one aim with absolute single-mindedness : the conquest of Constantinople. After seven years of siege the Turks took the town on May 29th, 1453. While the Turkish cannons threatened the Theodosian town wall on the western side, Mohamed sent his fleet to be transported overland to the Golden Horn. In his biography of Mohamed II, Franz Babinger describes the manœvers thus : 'The stretch of land from the narrowest part of the valley, now called the Dolma Bâghtsche, to the vine covered hills north of Pera and then downward to the present suburb of Qâsim-Pasha, was cleared with bundles of briar and covered with planks ; rails were provided at the steepest sections and the whole track was smeared with animal fat. Over this slipway, using barrels and rollers, the ships were pulled out of the Dolma Bâghtsche bay into the Golden Horn, seventy-two in all ; carrying full sail, with their crews cheering to the earsplitting accompaniment of kettledrums – filling the Christians with horrified astonishment — the ships slid into the foaming waters of the Golden Horn. When Mohamed entered the city, he rode straight to the Justinian Court Church of Hagia Sophia. He ordered the Islamic 'Creed' to be proclaimed from the pulpit, then himself mounted the altar steps and prayed with his face turned to Mecca. Hagia Sophia thus became an Islamic sanctuary.'

Until the reign of Beyazid I, the Ottoman rulers had called themselves 'Emir.' Beyazid replaced this with the more dignified title of Sultan. Before the conquest of Constantinople the name of the sovereign had always been invoked in the daily prayers as 'Sultan of the

Empire.' Mohamed, who now styled himself Fatih the Conqueror, had the prayer reformulated : the Sultan was now referred to as Lord of Two Seas and Two Continents. From this it becomes clear how much Constantinople must have meant to him. Fringed by two seas and two continents, the city had appeared to him as the only place suitable for the sovereign of an Empire whose borders stretched from Persia to Hungary.

The conquest of Constantinople presented Mohamed II with problems quite unlike those confronting his forefathers at their hour of victory. He had to evolve a plan for his future dealings with the alien civilization now under his rule. Constantinople was a thousand-year old metropolis admired throughout the Western world as an intellectual and cultural center. Mohamed's biographers show that his ideal from earliest youth had been Alexander the Great. Even before his accession he is supposed to have made an intensive study of the life and campaigns of Caesar and Augustus. His aim was to found a World Empire larger and more powerful even than that of Rome. Contemporary documents as well as historical events suggest that Mohamed II considered the conquest of Byzantium as the first step, and Rome as the next. His attitude towards Christian religion and culture was hence understandably tolerant. He recognized that to gain power over races which had been centers of older religions and cultures he would gain more by familiarization and discussion than by exclusion. Italian scholars, Greek architects and chroniclers, Jewish doctors and Persian poets lived together at his court. With worldly sophistication he maintained contact with these people, at the same time broadening his knowledge. This liberal behavior gave rise to rumors in the defeated Balkans that he had been converted to Christianity. For the conqueror of Byzantium to have been 'defeated' by the city's cultural traditions was something

that Christians in the west must have dreamt about. A letter from Pope Pius II to Mohamed reveals Italy's concern over the Sultan's growing power. The attacks of the Turkish fleet on Venice, the landing in Apulia and the occupation of Otranto (1480) increased this concern. In the letter (which never reached its destination) the Pope wrote: 'A mere trifle can make you the greatest, most powerful and most famous of men. And this trifle ? No rarity – a few drops of water ('aquae pauxillum') and you are baptized. Turn to Christianity and accept the gospels. Having done this, no sovereign in the whole world can surpass you in fame or match your power. We shall hail you Caesar over the Greeks and the Orient, and what you now unjustly hold by force alone would become yours by right. The Roman Church will not oppose you if you tread the path of righteousness. Under these conditions you could easily win many Empires without shedding blood'. Mohamed's unprejudiced toleration and his dislike of religious extremes had a critical reception from orthodox Islamic sects, and also from his son and heir, Beyazid II. Yet until the end of his life, Mohamed remained impervious to criticism of his tolerance. When the Venetian artist Gentile Bellini painted his portrait, some of his followers protested vigorously, seeing in this an attack on the foundations of Islamic faith.

Mohamed died in 1481 at the age of fortynine. Secure in the knowledge of their supremacy, his sons and grandsons extended the boundaries of the Empire. By the middle of the sixteenth century, during the reign of Süleyman the Lawgiver, the frontiers extended from Austria to Mesopotamia, from Rumania, the Crimea and the Caucasus to the Indian Ocean.

One of the many Ottoman acquisitions that gained special importance over the years was the conquest of Egypt. This was achieved at the beginning of the sixteenth century, during the reign of Selim I, the grandson of Mohamed II.

With Egypt's defeat, the Ottoman Sultan also became the Caliph. The Turkish sovereign was now not only the leader of State and Army, but also the religious leader of Islam, the representative of the prophet, the guardian of the Koran. Initially, the acquisition of the Caliphate was only significant in relation to foreign policy, but gradually it came to dominate the religious and economic development of the country. Soon after the death of Mohamed II, religious tolerance vanished. Beyazid II, a dedicated Mohammedan, quickly purged the court of 'foreign elements.' With the Caliphate, the Islamic tradition finally triumphed. Mohamed had dreamed of becoming the successor to the Roman Caesar. He wanted to rule a world-wide Empire, hence his religious liberalism. His sons, however, concentrated on Islam, as is shown by their acquisition of the Caliphate, and destroyed their father's efforts to effect a rapprochement of East and West, Islam and Christianity. The Turkish Sultan, at once sovereign of the Empire and spiritual leader of Islam, was now considered an even more formidable enemy by the West. The unification of the Islamic World under Turkish leadership was to hinder any religious rapport between the Turks and the West for centuries to come.

Süleyman the Lawgiver

Following the capture of Constantinople, the long reigns of successive Sultans contributed a great deal to the development of the Empire. Mohamed II and his son, Beyazid, each reigned for thirty years. Süleyman reigned for forty years, and during this time the Empire underwent its greatest expansion. The war with Hungary ended in a Turkish triumph. Belgrade fell to them, Vienna was besieged. To the East, the armies advanced as far as Mesopotamia. The capture of Baghdad was one of the most important gains in the Eastern campaigns.

During the reign of Süleyman, Turkish fleets appeared in the Western Mediterranean and were a power to be feared – attacks on Venice were followed by those on Southern Italy, Corsica and Sicily, and Rhodes and North Africa became occupied territories.

Süleyman's real achievement, however, lay in a flair for organization and administration. His ability to recognize talent in every walk of life, his skill in placing people in positions best suited to their gifts, made his reign the most famous epoch of the Ottoman Empire. His patronage in the field of architecture considerably surpassed that of his forefathers. In many respects, his reign may be compared with that of Justinian. Both of them ruled over approximately the same lands. In the mid-sixteenth century, an Eastern fleet threatened the western Mediterranean, ten centuries after Byzantine fleets had held sway over the same territories. Both Emperors were active legislators. Many contemporary documents testify that Justinian had personally taken part in the editing of the Corpus Juris. The Turks called Süleyman 'Kanuni' – the lawgiver. Both Emperors were forceful enough to revive what was traditional but also formulate new laws. During the reign of Justinian, Constantinople was transformed into the first Christian world capital. A thousand years later, Ottoman architects superimposed on the Byzantine city a completely different oriental Islamic capital: Turkish Istanbul. At Justinian's command, the Church of Holy Wisdom, Hagia Sophia, was built. In 536, it was dedicated with the words 'O Solomon, I have surpassed you.' Now, a thousand years later, Süleyman ordered his architect Sinan to design a mosque that would surpass Justinian's majestic church.

After Süleyman's Death

Süleyman's political power was so widespread that after his death its effects lingered on for almost another century. In 1683 Vienna was besieged unsuccessfully for the second time, and this marked the beginning of the Turkish withdrawal from central Europe. Battles with Austria and Hungary, action to suppress rebellion in the Balkans, were no longer campaigns of conquest. From 1683 onwards the role of the army changed. Now it acted only to preserve the status quo.

During this time architectural development took a similar turn. Süleyman's son, Selim II, was the last patron of the now aged Sinan. At the beginning of the seventeenth century the last great Sultan's mosque, the Ahmet Mosque, was built in Istanbul. The series of great mosques which began with that of Beyazid, reached its climax with Süleyman's building.

Revolts of the subject races, further wars in both East and West, and above all, mutiny amongst the Janissary presented the State with serious problems. After Süleyman's death, the Vizier Sokullu played an important role. The Empire owes its continued existence over several decades to him and several other far seeing statesmen. Court cabals, disputes over succession and fratricide hastened the fall of the House of Osman. In the context of this book we need not delve any further into the political and sociological reasons for this decline. The fact that the Ottoman Empire, from its first setbacks in the West to its final collapse in 1918, continued to survive for more than two centuries testifies to the deep-rooted strength of the heritage that Mohamed II passed on to Süleyman.

The subjects to be considered in the following chapters are (a) the Mosque as a sacred building ; (b) the Külliye, the whole complex of mosque and adjoining school and public buildings ; (c) the structure of the Turkish house. We are chiefly concerned with trying to understand and describe Turkish architecture as a whole. A chronological account of the development of Turkish architecture in isolation would be out of place. To understand its fundamental nature, we must distinguish between it and other Islamic architectural styles as well as Christian styles. We shall therefore deal mainly with the two significant phases of Turkish architecture ; its beginning and its zenith. Its beginning shows the break with what was traditional, and its flowering provides us with perfect examples of its highly distinctive style. The first phase includes the buildings of Bursa, while the second covers Sinan's work as Süleyman's Court Architect.

This study of the larger of the Sultan's mosques ends with a consideration of Sinan's last work, the Selim Mosque at Edirne. However, this does not mean that after Sinan's death no buildings of significance were erected. The Ahmet Mosque, completed in 1616, and the Yeni-Valide Mosque in Istanbul dominate the face of the city today. However perfect these mosques are, they do not reveal new architectural forms, but rather reflect variations on the basic forms created and elaborated by Sinan.

Domestic architecture was, however, a different matter. Practically no houses or palaces of the corresponding period survive today. The characteristic timbering and framework of domestic architecture condemned it to be short-lived, compared with the religious buildings which were built of stone. This also applies to the palaces. Ottoman sovereigns did not live in massive castles, but in a series of partition-like inter-connected rooms, hidden in green parks behind high walls. Our examples of domestic architecture must therefore be drawn mainly from the last two centuries.

Plates

Edirne (Adrianople)

21 **The Külliye of Beyazid II.** General view of the grounds from the south. In the foreground: the hospital and lunatic asylum wing.

22 Front façade of the mosque, seen from the forecourt.

23 Stalactite detail on the base of the minaret. As can be seen on plate 24, the minaret rises from a polygonal socle. The sides of this socle take the form of blind arcades. The arches have the simple form found in the early buildings of Bursa. The half-columns (cf. plate 24), which compose the sides of the polygon, form simple, straight lines between base and capital.

24 The mosque, seen from the south. The low building in the foreground is the southern medrese wing, a simple, square edifice with nine transoms topped by cupolas.

25 View from the north minaret, looking south. In the foreground: the cupolas of the forecourt of the mosque. In the middle distance, to the left, the courtyard between the hospital and the asylum; to the right, the asylum wing and its front garden. In the background, to the right, the Medical School.

26 View of the asylum wing, seen from the north west.

27 The large cupola in the middle of the picture belongs to the central hall of the hospital, hexagonal in shape.

28 The lunatic asylum.

29 The hexagonal hospital building, with the polygonal balcony on the river side. At high tide the river used to rise to the level of the mosque's foundation walls. Later on, the stretch of land lying between the Külliye and the river was filled up with earth. Nowadays the ground level in the hospital is lower than the level of the land surrounding the building.

30 View from the south minaret on to the roof of the hospital.

31 The central hall in the hospital. To the left and right, the cubicles occupied by the sick. In the middle axis, the small balcony (cf. plate 29).

32 A view into one of the adjoining rooms. The door on the right leads into the adjoining ward. There is no direct connection joining the sick rooms to the hexagonal central hall.

Istanbul

33 **The Mosque of Süleyman I.** View of the south-west façade of the mosque. In the foreground, the cupolas and chimneys of the western double-medrese.

34 The south-west façade, with side-entrance.

35 Detail of the south-east vestibule.

36 The buttresses on the south-east façade.

37 Detail from center of plate 36: a cluster of stalactites, the two corner buttresses join together to form a massive corner tower.

38 View from minaret of side cupola and large, stepped arcaded arch on side of mosque.

39 Entrance to the forecourt.

40 The interior of the mosque. View toward the south-east wall, with the mihrab.

41 Cupola and vaulted construction of the east corner.

42 A stalactite-filled 'pendentive' between two inner-sides of arches (detail from plate 41). The black outlines relate to recent renovation.

43 View on to the double medrese on the south-west side. The narrow passage between the two entirely symmetrical medreses joins the enclosure to the town.

44 Interior courtyard of the hospital.

Süleyman Mosque
Longitudinal and cross sections, plan, façade (section) 1:1000 and perspective 1:2000

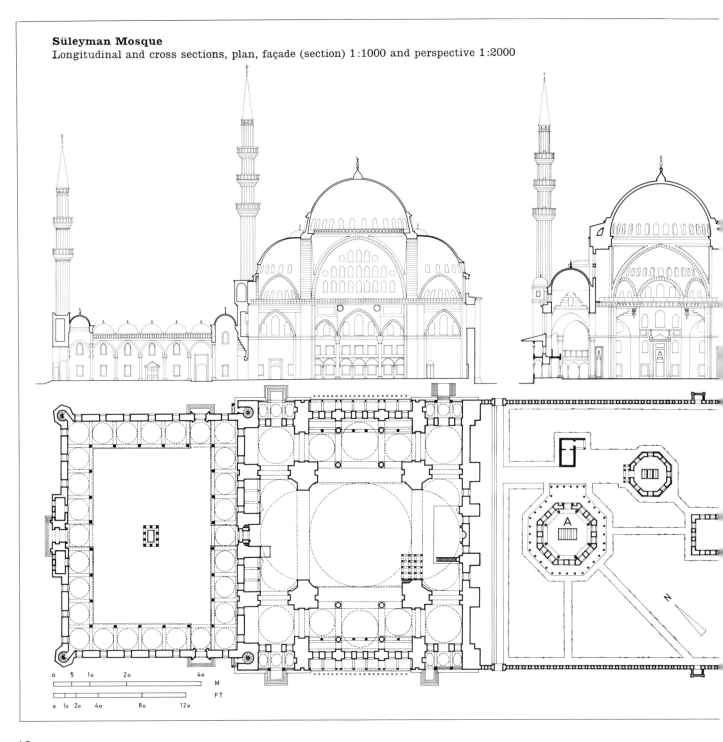

o 5 1o   2o   4o
                                M
                                FT
o 1o 2o   4o   8o   12o

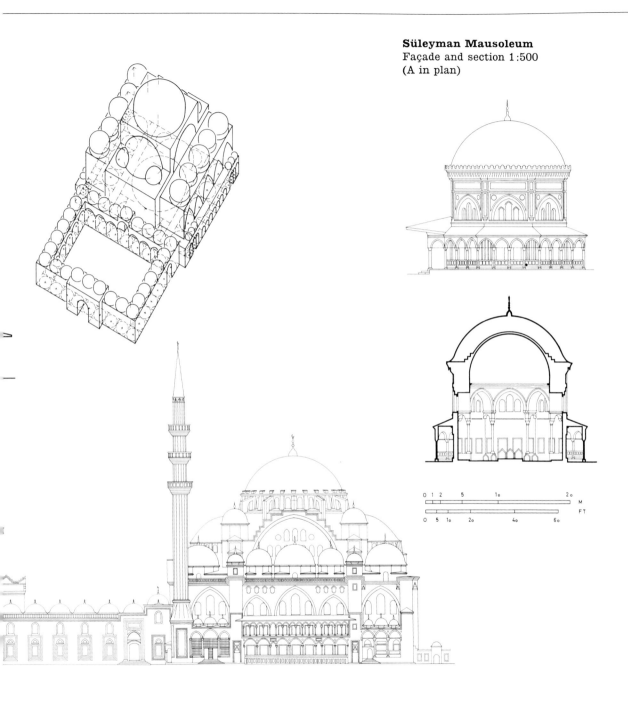

Süleyman Mausoleum
Façade and section 1:500
(A in plan)

Notes

Mosque Interiors

Kibla, the direction of Mecca, decides the positioning of the mosque. In Western Turkey the mosques stand facing South East. The Kibla wall is given special emphasis in the interior plan by the Mihrab, a recess to which the Imam and congregration turn in prayer.

The Mihrab, like the main doorway, is always constructed in stalactite form. Even in the smaller, less ostentatious mosques the Mihrab recess is lined with tiles and rich decoration. On the right of the Mihrab stands the Mimber, the priest's chair, a throne-like seat with several steps, built of stone or wood.

Edirne

Beyazid II's Külliye on the banks of the River Tundscha. It is still difficult to ascertain whether Hayreddin, the architect who built Beyazid II's mosque in Istanbul, was also responsible for the Külliye, or whether it was conceived by Murad.

The plan of the complex as a whole is new, whereas the mosque is built according to the traditional cube shape. it shows no trace of the problems of the Byzantine cupola structure which had already been creeping into the design of Istanbul mosques for several decades. As well as the two usual Medreses, the complex includes a large medical school, connected with a lunatic asylum and hospital.

The Külliye was generally a foundation (Vakf) provided by the Sultans or their representatives. The founding of mosques or charity institutions was also, however, a prerogative of any well-to-do citizen. The gift did not stop at the founding of the building, but depending on its importance, an amount of property and real estate would be included. The income to pay for the upkeep of the building, and wages for the priests and laymen who served in it, came out of the interest from the adjoining properties. A charter published by the founder set out the aims of the donation.

By religious law such a Vakf could not be revoked. Once completed, the founder had no further say in its affairs. The foundation could be neither sold, given away, nor bequeathed. It was publicly administered under the supervision of the Kadi, the religious judge. In the early Ottoman Kingdom the administration of the Vakf was an extensive organization; it eventually became a government ministry in 1841.

Istanbul

Süleyman's Mosque and Külliye, built between 1551 and 1557, is one of the most important of Sinan's creations. The layout of the mosque, courtyards, cemetery and adjacent buildings was a strikingly original achievement in town-planning. Along with the kitchens, baths and medrese buildings, this mosque constitutes a self-contained and stately sector of the town; built on the crown of one of the highest hills on the western side of the Golden Horn, it dominates the town. The cemetery behind contains Süleyman's mausoleum and also holds the body of his wife, Haseck-Hurem-Sultan (Roxelane) who died in 1573.

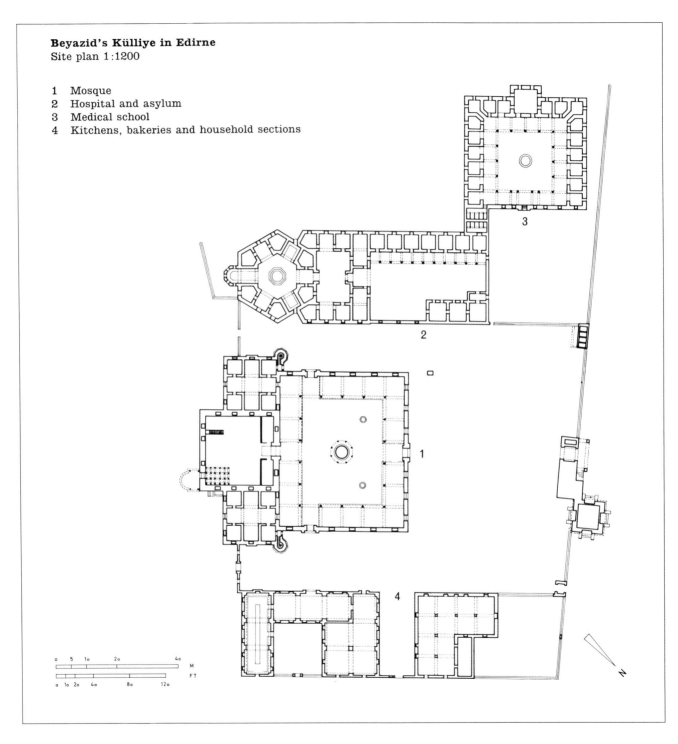

Beyazid's Külliye in Edirne
Site plan 1:1200

1 Mosque
2 Hospital and asylum
3 Medical school
4 Kitchens, bakeries and household sections

Beyazid's Külliye in Edirne
Façade (section), longitudinal section and plan of the medical wing 1:600

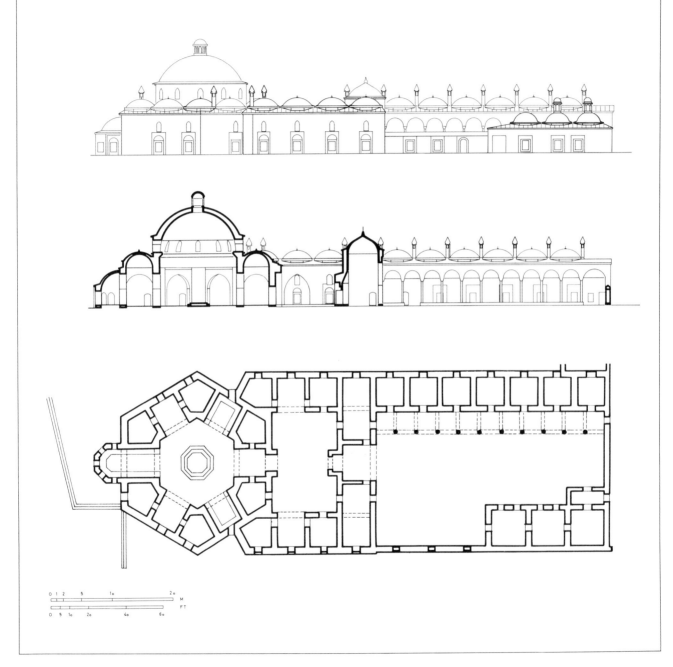

1. The Külliye or Complex of Mosque Buildings and its relation to the City as a whole

With the beginning and development of the Ottoman style of architecture in Bursa (1400-1460) a new tradition was born. Together with the mosque, the Sultan Orhan donated a Medrese or Theological School and a series of buildings for public use. Building a mosque and medrese interconnected, or in close proximity, was an ancient Islamic tradition, though the addition of public buildings — hospital, library, lunatic asylum, baths and alms-kitchen as a unit, creating a small independent community within the city — was an innovation. In the Mongol and Seljuk towns, the medrese had acquired an importance equal to, if not greater than, the mosque. For centuries, leaders and viziers of these Empires competed with one another to build increasingly imposing medreses. The great ones in Baghdad, Samarkand and Tus bear witness to this. The Mongols and Seljuks had accepted the Sunnitian faith, while the Persians followed the Schutian religion. The Sunnitian leaders founded these monumental medreses in Persia to emphasize their own beliefs.

The basic design of the Sunnitian medrese is an arcaded courtyard surrounded by small student cells, surmounted by domes and containing lecture halls at the four corners. The Sunnitian doctrine admitted four separate interpretations of the Koran, so Seljuk schools had four lecture halls in the form of an open Ivan. The Ottomans accepted only one interpretation, that of Abu Hanifa, and consequently Ottoman medreses had only one lecture hall, usually situated opposite the main entrance. The extreme climate of the Anatolian plateau later compelled west-Seljukian architects to abandon the open arcaded courtyard in favor of a smaller covered courtyard surmounted by a dome. Some historians consider this covered courtyard to be the earliest form of the Ottoman mosque. The Ottomans, however, retained the open arcaded courtyard of the Persian-Seljuk medrese, although on a much smaller and simpler scale.

The medreses of Bursa, Edirne and Istanbul all
have open arcaded courtyards.

The first mosque-medrese complex
to be built in Bursa

The mosque of Murad I in Bursa, built between
1361-1389, is the oldest existing mosque of the
early Ottoman period. Here for the first time we
see an attempt to unite mosque and medrese
under one roof. However, this appears to have
been the only attempt, since no other example
exists in the whole history of Turkish architecture. The building has two storeys on its north,
west and south sides. The large central room
with its adjoining chapel is two storeys high,
and contains study rooms and student cells. At
first sight, the façades with their different-
colored layers remind one of late Byzantine
palace façades. The arrangement of façades with
their pointed-arch arcades, on the other hand,

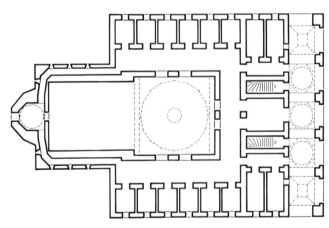

▲ The Mosque of Murad I in Bursa: Façade (after H.
Wilde) and groundfloor plan (after A. Gabriel)

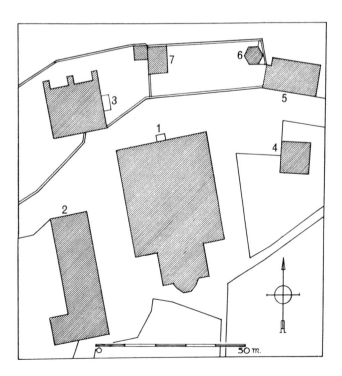

◄ The Külliye of Murad I: Site-plan (after A. Gabriel)

1 Mosque	4 Toilets
2 Alms-kitchen	5 School
3 Tomb	6–7 Summerhouse and Fountain

suggests Italian late-Gothic styles. The architect of this building was certainly neither Turkish, Persian, nor Byzantine, as early documents suggest. The Turkish traveler, Evliya Celebi, who explored the Empire in the mid-seventeenth century, noted in his diary that the architect must have been a 'Frank' (a European). The design, in any case, must have come from an artist who was well acquainted not only with Byzantine, but also Italian building traditions. Here for the first time we see the concept, as yet incomplete, behind the Külliye: to plan a mosque center, containing the Sultan's mausoleum and several other public buildings. Later plans were to include a hospital, lunatic asylum and a medical school.

The Yildirim – Beyazid Külliye in Bursa

The earliest example of a complete Külliye is that planned by Beyazid II in Bursa, and built between 1398-1403. This boldly-conceived building had been already started in Beyazid's lifetime, but Mongol attacks and the imprisonment and death of Beyazid himself interrupted the work. After his death, his son completed the Külliye, although its final form was not as grand as the original plan. The mosque and its surrounding buildings were damaged by an earthquake in 1855. The mosque alone was restored, and the medrese and other buildings are today mostly ruins. We learn from the Vakfiye, the Sultan's deeds of foundation, that the Külliye

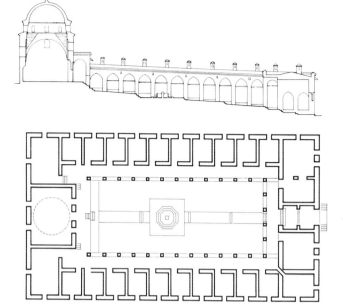

The Yildirim-Beyazid Külliye in Bursa ▶

Plan and section of the hospital (after A. Gabriel)

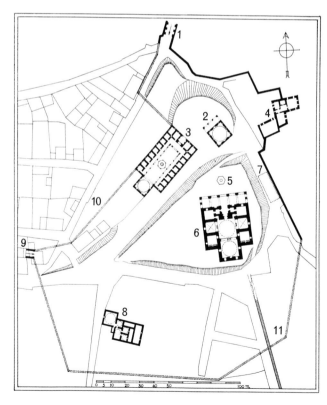

Site-plan (after A. Gabriel) ▶

1 Main entrance	5 Fountain	9 Side gate
2 Beyazid's Tomb	6 Mosque	10 Outer wall
3 Medrese	7 Alms-kitchen	11 Aqueduct
4 Harem	8 Hamam	

had also included besides the mosque, the medrese and the Sultan's mausoleum, a hospital, an alms-kitchen, a Dervish monastery, public baths and a Caravanseray.

The Yeschil-Cami Külliye in Bursa

This Külliye was founded by Mohamed I. Work started in 1403, and was completed after his death. Yeschil-Cami is the best preserved building in Bursa. The medrese, mausoleum, baths and alms-kitchen are still in excellent condition. Yeschil-Cami is the only Külliye in Bursa that gives us any conception of the entire design.

If one compares these three sites, one can see that similar locations have been chosen for each: a terrace-like slope on the outskirts of the city overlooking the vast plains of Bursa. No axis or parallels connect the different buildings with each other, no avenue leads directly to the main entrance of the mosque. In addition to its being the largest, most comprehensive building in the district, the mosque owes its dominance to its silhouette. Moreover, the topography of the region determined the positioning of the various buildings. The irregular curves determined the direction of the paths, and the buildings were then erected in relation to these. Because of this, and because the axis of the mosque had to face south-east towards Mecca, the grouping of the buildings on all three sites seems rather haphazard. The effect is emphasized by the distinctive style of the building. Initially, the Ottoman style, in contrast to the Seljuk style, was extremely simple, with few decorative elements. The mosque of Murad I, probably built by a foreign architect, is the only contemporary exception. Cubic forms, sharp corners and crystal-like polished stone are the basic elements of the new style. Cube and hemisphere comprise the geometrical forms of the rooms and also of the exterior surfaces. The absolute equality of the interior and exterior design is again a

significant trend, which from the beginning characterized Ottoman architecture. The grouping of simple geometrical cuboid buildings, dependent on the geographical nature of the locality, produced an effect of contrast. The stricter the geometrical form and the simpler the cube, the more picturesque appears the whole.

The building of huge medreses had been a long-standing tradition among Turkish tribes in the Near East. With the advent of Ottoman architecture in Bursa this tradition was abandoned. In the new Külliye designs the medrese lost its traditional architectural significance. The once purely religious building was transformed into a functional structure that became part of the other public buildings grouped around the mosque.

A similar change can also be observed in the architecture of the tomb: 'The most beautiful tomb is that which disappears from the earth's surface' – this saying of Mohamed has been strictly adhered to by Islamic races. The cult of the individual was objectionable to the Islamic race, particularly the building of statues or monuments. Only the early Turkish and Mongol leaders disregarded this tenet of their religion. The nomadic Turkish tribes, who in part had been forcibly converted to Islam, held on to their old customs for centuries. The mausoleum of Timur-Lenk in Samarkand, the tower-tombs in East Persia and the monumental cupola-tombs in Merchhed and Tus still stand today in the desert wastes of the Near East like huge petrified nomadic tents. The Ottoman leaders who represented the most orthodox stream of the Sunnitian sect broke with this old tradition. The Sultan's tomb, as well as those of his relations and followers were, even in the heyday of the Empire, small unobtrusive edifices surmounted by a cupola, to be found in the shadow of the mosques they had founded.

The tomb of Murad I is a simple four-sided structure which lies beneath the mosque, as does that of Beyazid I. The only tomb that is worthy of the name of monument is the Yeschil mausoleum, the grave of Mohamed I in Bursa. It is the only mausoleum erected in the Ottoman style that stands by the mosque, challenging it in size and artistic importance. The mausoleum lies behind the mosque on a higher terrace, thus dominating its surroundings. This edifice is significant in the history of Turkish tomb building not only because of its location and size, but also because of the beautiful decorated tiles it displays. Its interior and exterior are decorated with green glazed earthenware motifs. With the gradual acceptance of the Külliye, the Turkish tradition of tomb building disappears. After the capture of Constantinople, the tomb lost its significance completely.

The Külliye of Mohamed II in Istanbul

After the capture of Constantinople, the Külliye gained greater importance. The first Külliye in Istanbul was erected by Mohamed II on the site of the Justinian Apostolic church. This had contained the tomb of Justinian and his wife Theodora, and Mohamed now selected this site for his mosque, mausoleum and medreses. The mosque was built between the group of buildings comprising the medrese and was rather small and modest. Four large and four smaller units of the medrese bounded the mosque garden on the north-east and south-west sides. This domination of the medreses is, however, purely numerical – they present no architectural innovation; in fact quite the contrary. The simple basic schemes of the earlier medreses in Bursa were made even more simple and logical, because rooms were grouped into eight large and eight smaller units. The medrese cells with their low cupolas form two rows stretching away on the right and left sides of the mosque. They are

low, horizontally placed cubes and in no way compete with the mosque. Indeed they even emphasize its relative smallness. On the south-east side of the mosque garden, separated from it by a narrow path, we find the kitchens, alms-kitchens, baths and an inn. These secondary buildings were intended chiefly for the use of the students, and were organized so that the residential students could have as enjoyable a life as possible. The principle of the grouping of the buildings seems to have changed with this Külliye. The mosque becomes the main axis, and on the right and left sides are school buildings in symmetrical order. Here for the first time we see the conscious siting of the main building, the gradation of several other buildings according to their rank, and the differentiation of the sacred buildings and the utilitarian structure.

▼ The Külliye of Mohamed II in Istanbul
Site-plan (after A. -S. Ülgen)

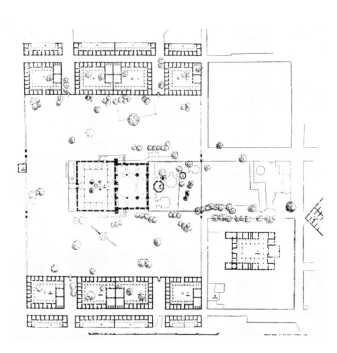

The Külliye of Beyazid II in Edirne (1484-1486)

Here the hospital, and not the medrese, is the most interesting feature. The building is situated on the banks of the River Tundscha, and the architect had a flat and wide area on which to work. The tradition of building the sovereign's tomb on the south-east side of the mosque, in the garden, had been started with the mosque of Mohamed II in Istanbul. At the same time Beyazid II ordered the building of a mosque and garden in the Medrese at Istanbul, where he intended to place the Sultan's tomb. Hence the Külliye at Edirne did not have a mausoleum garden. The architect now had the opportunity to move the Kibla wall right down to the banks of the river. Seen from the river, the mosque appears completely isolated, dominating the surrounding region with its beauty and tranquillity.

Low, small wings on either side of the building emphasize the perfect cube of the design. Two wings form the medrese: they are square in outline, and each wing is surmounted by nine small cupolas. These were used as theology schools, whereas the larger medrese, which together with the hospital and the lunatic asylum formed the right wing of the site, contained the medical school. A second collection of buildings on the north side separates the Külliye from the city. This left wing contained the alms-kitchen, dining rooms, bakeries, warehouse and workshop. Both wings extend parallel to the axis of the mosque, together with its forecourt they form a large square. This is separated from the street by a high wall containing a beautiful gateway.

The hospital wing which contained the hospital itself, the lunatic asylum and medical school, deserves special attention. A small inner covered courtyard connects the hospital and lunatic asylum and housed the pharmacy for both, plus the administrative offices. The hospital is an octagonal building with a central hall surmounted by domes. At a lower level, six closed hospital wards and five niches serving to enlarge the space, surround this marble hall. The lunatic asylum is, however, quite different. The wing is formed by seven cells, reached through a single portico. The hospital's octagonal outline, the central hall and the open wards set in the form of an Ivan made for easy contact between patients and convalescents, whereas cells in the asylum were isolated from one another, and could only be reached via the portico.

Evliya Celebi describes this design very accurately in his diaries. He was particularly impressed by the treatments given to patients, especially the attempts made to cure insanity by means of music. The airy open spaces and gardens of the lunatic asylum were also admired by the diarist. It is interesting to note that even five hundred years ago, music and nature were used for therapeutic purposes. Also interesting is the combination of medical school and hospital, thus simultaneously offering students both theory and practice. On a purely architectural level, this unit was excellently designed, as can be seen in the grouping of the various rooms and the different character given to each. A small path connects the medical school with the lunatic asylum garden. The medrese shows the customary design of inner court, student cells and a central lecture hall. We learn from the Vakfiye that a large medical staff had been employed. One medical superintendent, two head physicians, two opticians, two surgeons and one pharmacist are mentioned, in addition to some hundred and fifty other employees.

Süleyman's Külliye in Istanbul

In 1550, with great ceremony, the foundation stone of the mosque and Külliye, designed by

▲ Süleyman's Mosque in Istanbul
(after a woodcut by M. Lorich)

Sinan, was laid. Süleyman had intended that this building should surpass not only those of his Byzantine predecessors but also those of his own ancestors. The program called for numerous buildings: two double medreses, one hospital, one caravanseray, one medical school and a hamam (baths). Sinan conceived this vast undertaking very differently from the architects of Edirne, Murad and Hayreddin. The latter had had a flat stretch beside a river on which to build. The site chosen for Sinan's design was the third hill along the Golden Horn, the most dominant area of the city. The distance between the mosque and the other buildings now becomes considerably greater. The mosque rises in isolation, set in gardens enclosed by low walls. Sinan placed the other buildings opposite, where they run parallel to the gardens. The medical school and alms-kitchen are opposite the main entrance of the mosque; the hospital and the caravanseray are on the corner to the right of the entrance. A medrese is placed on both sides of the street. Only the mausoleums of the Sultan and his wife, Hasseki-Hurem, are in the immediate vicinity of the mosque in the back garden.

At first sight, Sinan's reasons for placing the medrese and the other buildings in this order are not clear. At the Külliye's north-west corner the alms-kitchen, medical school and hospital form a completely enclosed area; the north-east corner and the other side of the northern street are partially undeveloped. Only at the level of the mosque does the northern group of medreses begin. Because of the obligatory south-east axis, the mosque's main entrance had to be to the north-west. The harbor, the town center and the Sultan's harem were therefore south-east of the mosque. Because of this, the main entrance to the Külliye is only reached from the town by making a detour. Sinan erected a number of buildings to complete the detour, thus providing an avenue leading to the mosque.

A woodcut by Melchior Lorich, executed three years after the mosque's completion, shows that the east corner of the site was then also undeveloped. The mosque stands in the center of the site and emphasizes the Külliye's main axis. The other buildings are grouped in a rectangle around the mosque. Entering the Külliye from the town one sees the mosque from its east side and is not immediately aware of its axial design. Its form only becomes apparent when one has walked along the west side of the street. However, the alleys that lead to the main entrance of the mosque are so designed that the full frontal view of the mosque appears only at the last moment. The cemetery garden behind the mosque where the mausoleum of Süleyman and his wife stands, is similar in design. Although the Sultan's grave lies on the mosque's main axis, one cannot see this when entering the cemetery, for the porch bypasses the mausoleum, instead of leading directly to the entrance. In fact, the entrance hall runs parallel to the path. The Sultan's wife's tomb lies at the end of the same path, but its entrance is also at the side.

Architecturally it is a fact that the use of a long avenue leading to the façade of a building emphasizes its impact. The emphasis on axial direction has been used in architecture since Egyptian times as a means of stressing solidity and endurance. The cemetery here reveals a characteristic of Turkish architecture which stems from a religious attitude. The grave being only the temporary house of the corpse, its design or structure should in no way give an impression of permanence. It was merely a place of remembrance, not of worship. Not only was this belief a basic tenet of the Islamic faith, but as we shall see, it also became basic to the planning and construction of Turkish towns.

During the early epoch in Bursa, we have seen that there was no set plan for the grouping of buildings; they were adapted to the geographical formation of the region. The Külliye of Beyazid II in Edirne, however, is one of the earliest sites where the emphasis rests on the mosque's central position. In Sinan's work, this hierarchical order of mosque and adjacent buildings became even more pronounced. Sinan's plan for the internal organization of the utilitarian buildings is perfect, and they are, in relation to the mosque, extraordinarily simple. As Sinan's designs for the mosque increased in complexity, so his plans for the surrounding buildings became more modest. The outlines of the medreses and alms-kitchen were simplified in inverse proportion to the innovations in the design of cupolas and the system of supports this engendered. The artistic achievement of Sinan's Külliye is to be found in his grouping of the various architectural units. Designs for the medreses, caravanseray and hospitals are not, however, outstanding innovations. In some cases Sinan reduced the architectural significance of the medrese to such an extent that the cells are grouped around the courtyard of the mosque; thus the medrese became a mere fore-hall of the mosque (as in the mosques of Sokullu, Mihrimah and Kara-Ahmet).

The reason why designs for medreses did not develop to the same extent as those for mosques during the Ottoman era is certainly due to the Külliye system, which was an Ottoman innovation. It originated from two divergent trends: on the one hand, it is a manifestation of growing imperial power; on the other, it results from the personal ambitions of the founders who wished to surpass the efforts of their predecessors. The two trends achieved a balance in the erection of public buildings. The greater the pretensions to power, the greater the urge became to found such buildings. This balance between ambition and altruism finds its finest expression in the Külliye system.

The Turkish Town

Over the centuries two factors are significant in the structure of Turkish towns: the Turks' nomadic origins, and their later conversion to Islam. In some spheres the two factors came into conflict, but in matters of architectural planning they complemented each other. The Islamic doctrine has always been strongly against the over-rating of the material world. An object is there to be used; a means to an end, but never an end in itself. In his 'History of Town Planning' (Vol. II), Ernst Egli remarks that whenever a town is mentioned in the Koran it is only in a negative sense – indeed towns are repeatedly connected with the idea of destruction. Nowhere are the rebuilding or development of towns valued per se. Egli finds an explanation for this in Arab tradition. By nature nomads – although they were later to conquer vast continents – the Arabs were never in a position to settle down and found large towns. While a town did provide them with a place for communal worship and activity, it nonetheless never became a permanent home. The town is a world in itself, planned, built and organized by men, a place of which its creators may be proud. Ancient towns and cities, especially the Roman ones, were not only residential centers, but also permanent monuments to mankind. It is precisely this which the Koran warns against.

'If your fathers and your sons and your brothers and your wives and your relations and the substance which you have acquired and the trade which you fear to lose, and if your dwellings wherein you delight be more dear to you than God and his prophet and the advancement of his Kingdom, then wait until God come at the final judgment.' (9/24)

'Woe to the loose-tongued slanderer, who heaps up riches and counts them again and again. He thinks that riches have made him immortal. On the contrary, he will surely soon be cast into the realms of damnation.' (104. 2/3/4/5)

The Koran states more than once that the destruction of towns through natural catastrophe is the result of God's anger. It is seen as an apocalyptic warning to rouse men from worldly forgetfulness. The town and its development are interpreted very negatively; once founded, a town's very existence tempts its citizens to greater ambition: property will tend to accumulate in the hands of individuals or a small section of the community. Earthly goods are condemned as a negative acquisition. Wealth and earthly power can only be justified if shared out among the poor.

Once this is understood, we progress to a deeper appreciation of the idea behind the Külliye. A new problem must now be considered. With the increasing prosperity of the Empire, the Külliye became more numerous. The Sultan and his relatives were joined by statesmen and wealthy citizens in the competition to donate public buildings. This was certainly a sign of prosperity. At the same time, we cannot but wonder at the widespread poverty in the Empire at a time of such charitable activity. Again the Koran tenders an explanation: according to Islamic belief, wealth is not a virtue nor a badge of distinction any more than poverty is attributed to incompetence or social inferiority. By giving, the rich man justifies his wealth in the sight of God and his fellow beings, and although by doing so he is creating a monument, he is remembered only as a benefactor.

Traditionally nomads, the Turks were by nature ready to embrace the Islamic faith. The tent was easily moved from one place to another. Neither sovereign nor soldier, rich nor poor, owned permanent property. Even later, when the Turks had settled and built cities, this basic attitude remained unchanged. There is, for example, an unusual quality of uniformity in their domestic buildings, both in size and material. Timber was predominant; stone was rarely used, being usually reserved for the mosques and Külliyes. One can visualize the average Turkish town as a straggling haphazard collection of wooden buildings, surrounding patches of green vegetation. Trees were not allowed to grow in squares or streets, but flourished in gardens hidden behind high walls. The unobtrusive and repetitive exteriors of the buildings created a certain monotony – even the palaces of the Sultans and the nobility are no exception. In contrast to Western Renaissance or Baroque palaces, the residences of the Ottoman sovereigns and statesmen are extremely modest. If we compare the design of a Turkish town with that of a contemporary European town, differences at once stand out: wide straight streets and any organized network of roads and squares are conspicuously absent. In fact the purpose of a Turkish street was none other than a means of communication through a labyrinth of houses. Often it was merely an entry to the house, for between this jumbled collection of houses one often comes across blind alleys. Squares, when they exist, are large open areas, used on market days, and never become a town center, as do market squares in Western towns. Trading streets are also rarely found, since the bazaar, with its barrel-vaulted streets, constituted the shopping center of the Turkish town. Squares were not built as a meeting place for the citizens, just as streets had none of the features of the Italian 'corso' or promenade. Moreover, the European concept of a main road for parades and processions does not exist in the old Turkish town. Consequently, streets and squares were less cared for, and the European traveler is continually surprised by the cultivated gardens and lavish homes hidden behind insignificant wooden façades in rough narrow streets.

Within the network of roads and houses, the mosque and its Külliye formed a separate district. In European cities, larger buildings, like hospitals, schools, hotels or public baths, are to be found widely scattered round the town. They become the focal point of a street, or lend individuality to a district. In the Külliye, all these buildings were grouped around the mosque, and together with the latter, they constitute a well-proportioned unit set among wooden houses and irregular clumps of trees.

The Significance of Water and Greenery in the Turkish Town

The Islamic faith originated in the desert; the heritage of the Turks was that of the steppes. Both were arid and shadowless landscapes. The lack of water and scarcity of trees resulted in the Islamic concept of paradise. In the Koran, running streams and trees are continually equated with paradise. For Islam, water signifies the origins of life: rain is God's most precious gift. The image of water as the essence of life has always been important to the Turks.

It was certainly not accidental that, as soon as they had established themselves politically, the Turks turned their attention to the capture of the Byzantine town of Brussa (Bursa). To the former inhabitants of the desert, this 'green' town, as it was later called, must have seemed paradise.

The Austrian historian, Hammer-Purgstall, travelled to Bursa and Nikea in 1804. He described these towns in glowing terms: 'Everywhere one can see springs and fountains of cold and warm water; they spurt from rocks, they trickle from walls, they flow along canals and through pipes, they ripple and wind along the ground and streets in all directions. They flow artificially upward in pipes to descend naturally in waterfalls; they sprinkle the garden lawns, they settle the dust.'

Turkish sovereigns had three opportunities to transform a conquered Christian town into a new capital: Bursa, Adrianople and Constantinople. Each of these towns represented a new stage of development in the early Ottoman Empire. Although relatively close to one another, the geographical positions of the towns are quite different: Bursa (Brussa) is situated near the Olymp, a mountain range in Asia Minor, whose summits are snow-covered until spring. Edirne (Adrianople), a town set in flat countryside, is watered by the rivers Meric, Arda and Tuna. The area is hot, dry and sparsely vegetated. Finally, Istanbul (Constantinople): a city by the sea. Water played an especially significant part in the urbanization of the landscape in Bursa and Istanbul, although in different ways.

Bursa

The old Byzantine citadel was built on a hill, in accordance with the customs of the time. After its conquest, Orhan set up his residence in the old citadel. The first Turkish mosque and baths were erected during his reign within the walls of the old Byzantine fortress. West of the old town walls, on higher ground, Murad II built his mosque with its imposing cemetery garden, in which the tombs of his wives and children were placed next to his mausoleum. Later the town spread to the east and north-east. The first residential area developed to the east of the citadel, with a huge mosque, the Ulu-Cami, dominating the surroundings. The Ulu-Cami was not a Sultan's mosque, but a city mosque erected for the citizens' daily use. It was a master product of three generations; founded during the reign of Murad I, continued under Beyazid I, it was finally completed under Mohamed I, the founder of the Yeschil-Cami Külliye. A simple building without forecourt or hall, it contains arcades and is surmounted by twenty small domes and two low minarets.

The Turkish Sultans built their Külliye on the

outskirts of the town. As we have noted, the Külliyes of Murad I, Beyazid I and Mohamed I were built on sloped terraces. If we examine the architecture of the city, we see that a similar plan was used here. The town was not built according to a preconceived plan; rather, its natural surroundings determined the way in which it grew, and dictated the sites of the Sultans' mosques. It is difficult to understand why these mosques were sited as they were. They are at some distance from the citadel, the former residence of the Sultans, and no direct route connects the Külliye with the Palace. The right-angle of the plans seems to have been left out intentionally. Streaming down from the Uludag (the Mount Olympus of Asia Minor) the River Gokdere bisects the town in a north-easterly direction. A maze of narrow lanes and blind alleys run along the slopes of the two hills. Thus the siting of the Sultans' mosques did not arise logically from the ground-plan of the city. Their significance is seen from the steppes; viewed in profile, it becomes clear that they form an intentional counterpoint with the old citadel.

An imperial palace in the form of a castle built on a hill was foreign to Turkish thought. The early Ottoman Sultans of Byzantium had another solution; although unaware of the significance of their action, they de-centralized their towns by moving their residences, mosques and mausoleums to the outskirts. Thus the old pattern of city-planning gradually underwent a transformation.

The Special Site of Istanbul

The city was originally named Byzantium; this changed to Constantinople, and finally to Istanbul. Founded by the Greeks, and developed by the Romans, it became a capital city, and for over a thousand years remained the metropolis of the Roman Empire of the East. For a further five hundred years, the city was the capital of the Ottoman Empire. With its key position, holding 'two continents and two seas,' the city was ideally placed for both the Byzantine sovereigns and the Ottoman Sultans.

The structure of the city has always been governed by its geographical position between the Sea of Marmara and the Golden Horn. The hills have proved especially significant. The harbor, main streets and main gates have remained unaltered since Roman times. The city's monuments, however, have undergone a series of changes – just as Greco-Roman gave way to Byzantine, so the latter were replaced by Turkish. The Justinian Churches of St. Sophia and Irene were built on the foundations of ancient Byzantine temples. After the Turkish conquest, the great Justinian Church of the Apostles, modeled on St. Mark's in Venice, made way for a mosque. Many cities, such as Rome, have experienced a similar fate. Like present-day Istanbul, Rome has received its modern face from sixteenth and seventeenth century buildings. But while these buildings, relics of different epochs, have survived side by side, those in present-day Istanbul have to some extent been superimposed on one another. Today Istanbul presents an essentially Turkish aspect. The Church of St. Sophia, built over the earlier Acropolis of Byzantium, can, when viewed from a distance, barely be distinguished from the other mosques. Turkish architects added four minarets, a Medrese and library buildings to the original church, and consequently it merges well into the skyline of the Turkish city.

The Greek settlement in Byzantium was confined to the spit of land (today the Palace Point) between the Sea of Marmara and the Golden Horn. A wall extended from the south-west side of what is now the Church of St. Sophia to the Golden Horn and formed the landward border of the city. After the Roman conquest, the city began to develop westwards beyond the walls of the Greek colony. The area between the walls of Greek Byzantium and the sea of Marmara was, from its inception, one of the most important focal points of the city. The new Roman city had for its center the Augusteion, erected between St. Sophia and the later Kara-Ahmet Mosque. The Augusteion was connected to the Hippodrome by its shorter, western side. On the long, southern side near the sea, magnificent palaces were later erected for the Byzantine Emperors. They, in turn, were replaced by the Kara-Ahmet

Mosque. The square in front of this mosque still reveals in its ground plan traces of the Hippodrome which once stood there.

From the Augusteion, the Mese, or main street of the Roman town, leads westwards to the Fora of Constantine and Theodosius. The present main street still follows the original Mese, running between the Church of St. Sophia and the Beyazid Mosque. A little further on, at the Forum Amostrianum the Mese forks into

▼ Istanbul (an engraving by A. Vavassore, c. 1500)

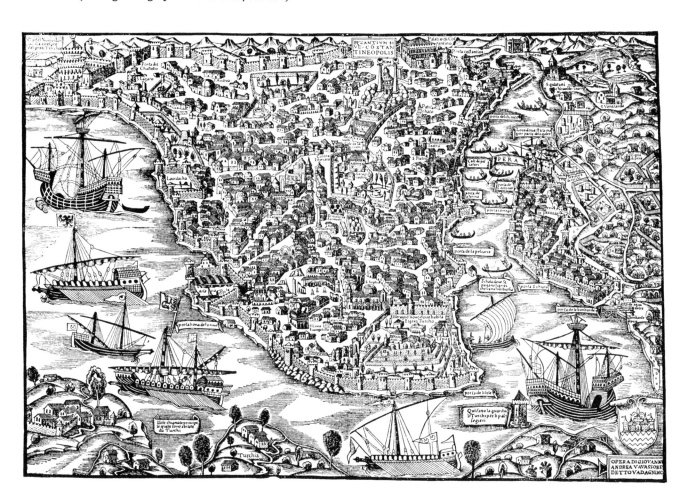

two main streets running respectively north-west and south-west. The south-west fork leads, via the Fora of Bovis and Arcadus, to the Porta Aurea, the Southern gate of Theodosius's city walls. From here, a street running parallel to the shore leads to Hebdamon, the summer residence of the Byzantine emperors. The north-west fork runs in an almost parallel direction to the Aqueduct of Valens (most of which is today still in good condition), and from there to the Charisios gate on the northern city wall. Today, the two main streets to Top Kapi and Edirne Kapi also follow the old routes of the north-western and south-western Mese.

During the Roman period the Mese was already lined with arcades and colonnades, and punctuated at intervals with fora. These squares were decorated with columns, triumphal arches and paintings. In the fora, and especially in the Hippodrome, was focused the political and social life of the time. Neither isolated temples, nor churches, but these boldly planned streets and open squares gave the Roman and Byzantine town its essential character. During the Turkish redevelopment of the city, the mosques became the focal points of the layout. Although the arterial roads remained the same, the Turks' municipal planning was completely at variance with that of Greco-Roman and Byzantine tradition.

The late-classical basilicas and fora were stereometrical ordered creations, whose façades also formed the inner walls of the magnificent public squares and processional streets. The squares of the town in its late Roman and Byzantine periods were centers from which radiated the chief thoroughfares. The Mese served mainly for ceremonial processions, which entered the town via the Porta Aurea. A tenth century Byzantine diary describes Justinian's entry into the city, and clearly indicates how vital a part streets had to play; and we can recognize in this a continuation of Roman tradition. This procession through the city, the triumphal march, are climaxes of communal celebrations familiar to ancient Rome. The street was not merely a means of getting from one place to another, but a medium through which the sovereign could come into contact with his people, and where different social strata met. Yet the Byzantines differed from the Romans (and Ottomans) in that they preferred to hold their ceremonial processions during the evening. A procession at night, the darkness pierced by flickering torches and candles, was the climax of a Byzantine festival—be it to celebrate a sovereign's entry, or a funeral: a contemporary Byzantine historian describes Justinian's funeral as taking place at night by candlelight. Similar descriptions of festive occasions have, however, not been found in any reports by Ottoman historians.

In 'Constantinople, Image of a Holy City,' Philip Sherrard draws attention to the fact that the shaping of Constantinople as the 'New Rome' was based on the image of Holy Jerusalem. Thus the Byzantines had no misgivings about indulging their taste for pomp and splendor, precious materials and gems. Their devotion to the heavenly city served to increase their passion for magnificence and extravagance in creating its replica. The Islamic doctrine, however, was diametrically opposed to this. As a result, Turkish architecture reserved its monumental splendor for sacred buildings. The growing power of the Turkish Sultans did not lead them to develop Istanbul in the rich Byzantine manner. As we have seen, the Turks had no home-loving roots and consequently they never erected splendid palaces or residences.

The shaping of Istanbul was also influenced by the Turkish concepts of communal life. The Roman and Byzantine concern to foster free discussion, political debate and entertainment in

◀ Constantinople: Plan showing the principle buildings and streets during the Byzantine period

1 Golden Gate	5 Church of the Holy Apostles
2 Mese	6 Taurus Forum
3 Arcadius Forum	7 Hippodrome
4 Bovis Forum	8 St. Sophia

public places was foreign to the Turks. The quiet courtyards and streets of the Külliye should never be compared with the agora or forum of ancient times. The Turks did not use the courtyards of the mosques as meeting places: they met in open-air cafes usually situated close to the mosque and beside a well, overhung by spreading plane trees. Theirs was not, therefore, an architecturally ordered square with a geometrically ordained position in relation to a network of roads, but a green tent in the shadows of a mosque. 'Here, at any hour of the day, people gathered together – lovers of nature and news, the inquisitive and the idle, talkers and listeners, the tired and lively, ill and healthy, natives and strangers, all rested on soft carpets and whiled away the hours in an atmosphere compounded of tobacco and the scent of coffee. Immersed in delightfully idle talk or even more delightful

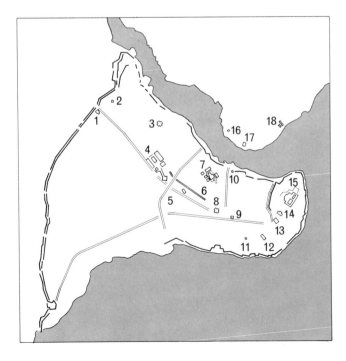

◀ Istanbul: Plan showing the principle buildings and streets during the Ottoman period

1 Mihrimah Mosque	10 Rustem Pasha Mosque
2 Chora Church	11 Sokullu Mosque
3 Selim Mosque	12 Sultan Ahmet Mosque
4 Mohamed II Külliye	13 St. Sophia
5 Şehzade Mosque	14 St. Irene
6 Valens Aqueduct	15 Top Kapi Seray
7 Süleyman Külliye	16 Azap-Kapi Mosque
8 Beyazid II Mosque	17 Rustem Pasha Han
9 Atik-Ali Mosque	18 Kilich Ali Mosque

dreams, they recline near the banks of the canal, watching the reflections of the white shining marble muted by those of the green leaves and blue sky.' Hammer Purgstall here describes a café in Bursa, but his description could apply to many an old café in other Turkish towns.

The municipal buildings that formed an essential part of the old Byzantium were already in ruins before the Turkish conquest, and were not rebuilt. Byzantine fora and squares were replaced by residential districts. Only the main streets today still follow the old Meses. The hill between the Golden Horn and the Sea of Marmara was put to a totally new use by the Turks. Following Roman tradition the Byzantines had built according to layouts and plans, whereas the Turks had an eye for the natural contours of the region when seen from the sea. This was the starting-point for the siting of the mosques. In this way they enhanced the city's natural silhouette with a unique architectural ornamentation of domes and minarets. What their predecessors had drawn horizontally in a design of squares and spacious streets, the Turks redesigned in vertical planes and silhouettes. The Külliye of Istanbul thus achieves additional architectonic significance. We have already observed that in Sinan's Külliye, the buildings around the mosque have been greatly simplified, in order to set off the soaring pyramid lines of the mosque as clearly as possible. His Medreses and alms-kitchen run horizontally, forming what appears from a distance to be a sort of socket for the mosque. Sinan and his successors achieved here a new architectural form that attained perfection in pure outlines set against the sky. Only in Constantinople did the mosque become a fundamental part of the city's silhouette; and in this it differs from other Islamic towns in Asia and Africa, where sacred buildings were built with much less regard for their relation to the city as a whole. Istanbul's location by the sea certainly contributed to this new conception of town-planning. From the architectural point of view, areas of water in Istanbul did not merely define the city's basic structure, as in many other harbor-cities. Here the surface of the sea was an infinite gleaming mirror that captured and reflected the precious filigree work of the outlines of the buildings, rising in tiers one above the other; and the soaring slender outlines are complemented by their shimmering reflections in the water below.

Plates

Bursa

67 **The Yeschil Mausoleum and Mosque.** View of the former Külliye from the South.

68 Interior of the Yeschil-Cami. The prayer room and the Mihrab on the south-east wall. The flat arched form is typical of early Ottoman architecture in Bursa. The use of the tambour as transition from square to circle is also typical. The lower half of the tambour can be seen in the foreground.

69 Inner walls of the Mihrab niche.

70 View of the Sultan's box situated on the second floor of the building and approached from the entrance hall.

71 View of the Stalactite dome. This dome is above the Sultan's box on the second floor. The dome, filled with stalactites, and the round openings in the shell of the dome, are rare in Ottoman mosques, and do not occur in later buildings in Istanbul.

Istanbul

72 **The Şehzade Mosque (the Princes' Mosque).**
73 The north-east façade. The highly decorative relief ornamentation on the lower half of the minaret and the sharp outlines on the upper part of the main building dies out in Sinan's later work.

74 General view of the mosque and forecourt, from the north-west.

75 The main façade of the forecourt.

76 Side entrance to the forecourt and the base of the north-west minaret.

77 Buttresses on the south-east façades.

78 **The Sokullu Mosque.** The mosque's forecourt and part of the main façade. The medrese cells are grouped round the courtyard in a similar way to those of the Mihrimah Mosque.

79 Well in the forecourt.

80 Interior of the mosque, looking towards the South-West wall. To the left, the tiled Mihrab wall with the Mimber.

81 Window in the upper part of the Kibla wall, seen from the interior.

82 View of the main dome. The Kibla wall stands out from the other contrasting white walls by means of the glowing colors of its tiles.

83 Detail of the Mihrab wall. In the lower left corner, part of the marble frame of the Mihrab niche. Upper right, the pointed tiled roof of the Mimber.

84 Upper part of the central arcade and the tiled pendentive between the two side half-domes.

85 View of the south-west wall, both side half-domes, and the central dome. The painting on the central dome dates from a subsequent restoration. Against the unpainted white side walls of the mosque, the stalactites stand out, expressing the 'freezing' of the downward stresses. This is rare example of the 'deductive' principle of building, passing from the large to the small, and a particular feature of Sinan's work.

86 Half-capital of a pillar connecting the outer wall and the gallery.

Yeschil-Külliye in Bursa
Site plan of the külliye 1:1500

1 Mosque
2 Mausoleum
3 Medrese

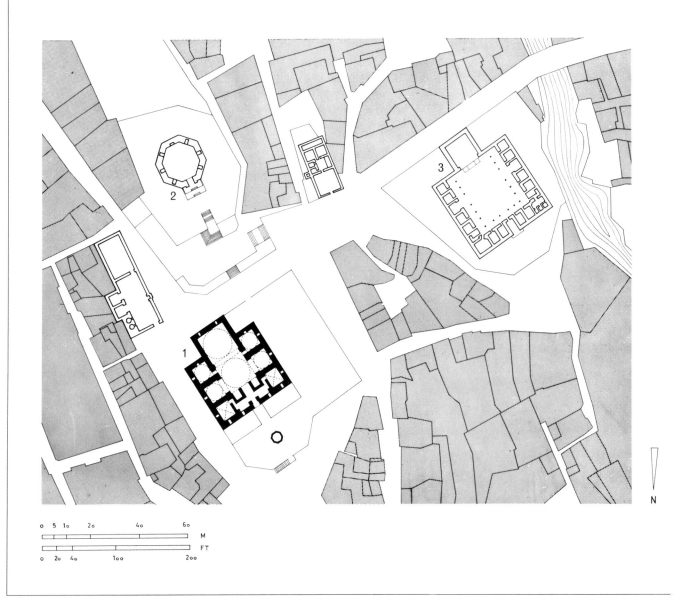

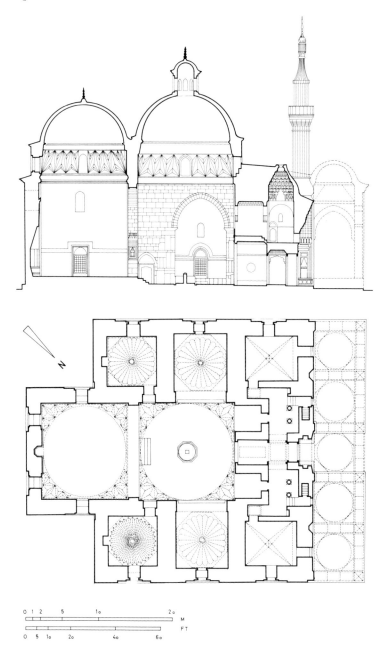

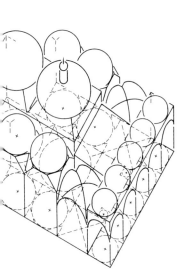

0 1 2   5   1o   2o
                                        M
                                        FT
0   5 1o   2o   4o   6o

Notes

Bursa

The Külliye of Mohamed I (The 'Green' Külliye), the Yeschil-Cami and the Yeschil Mausoleum (built in 1413-1421).

The Governor of Bursa, Hadschi-Ivaz Pasha, is mentioned in inscriptions in the mosque as its founder and builder. Frequent references to his name have given rise to the theory that he also originally designed the plans. Hadschi-Ivaz came to Bursa from Anatolia as a simple soldier, but rose rapidly to dazzling heights under Mohamed I, finishing his career as Vizier. A. Gabriel considers that while Hadschi-Ivaz most certainly originated the idea of the mosque, he was not in fact its architect. He is convinced that it was a Turkish architect who planned and dompleted the building under Ivaz Pasha's guidance. Celâl Esad gives the name of the architect as Ayas, without proving his assumption. Other literature on Bursa tends to name Iliyas-Ali as the architect. This artist decorated the building; he did not, however, design it. By all accounts, he came to Bursa from Täbriz at a time when the building was nearing completion. The work of decorating the building was carried out after its completion — which Mohamed I did not live to see (he died in 1421). The Yeschil Mausoleum also dates from this period.

According to descriptions by Evliya-Celebi, the dome and minaret had originally been decorated with colored tiles. But the earthquake which severely damaged both mosque and mausoleum destroyed the old minaret completely. The two minarets we see today date from the nineteenth century, and are exact replicas of the originals.

In 1864, the French architect, L. Parvillé, acting on the instructions of A. Vefik Pasha, at that time governor of Bursa, undertook to restore the mosque as completely as possible. He settled in Bursa for a number of years to supervize the restoration work. One of his sketches shows that the tambour was painted with leaf motifs and regular designs; this seems to have been a mistake — plant motifs and prismatically divided surfaces were always alternative, not combined, methods of decoration.

Istanbul

The Şehzade Mosque was build by Sinan under the rule of Süleyman I, between 1544-1548. This was the first large mosque to be built by Sinan in Istanbul. Süleyman had it erected to commemorate his two sons who both died at an early age. The Princes' mausoleums are in the garden behind the mosque. A departure from Sinan's usual strictly pared-down style of mausoleum, these two buildings are decorated with ribbed domes and colored stone.

The Şehzade Mosque reveals Sinan's contact with a new influence, that of the design of St. Sophia. Yet in this first effort, Sinan succeeded in achieving his most important new ideas.

Sokullu Mohamed Pasha's Mosque. This mosque, built by Sinan in 1571, was commissioned by the Grand Vizier, Sokullu. The Mosque, erected on a steep slope, combines with the medrese, laid out around the mosque's courtyard, to form one of Sinan's most satisfying designs.

The mosque's ground plan draws on earlier tradition. Sinairi Pasha's Mosque in Beschiktasch on the Bosporus, and the Kara-Ahmet Mosque in Istanbul, both built in 1555, served as preliminary experiments in the form later used in the Sokullu Mosque. Both have hexagonal central halls with two domes on each side. This early Turkish design, used in several minor mosques in West Anatolia and in the Uç Serefeli Mosque in Edirne, gave Sinan the idea for designing the central domed hall in a new style which did not draw on the techniques used in St. Sophia.

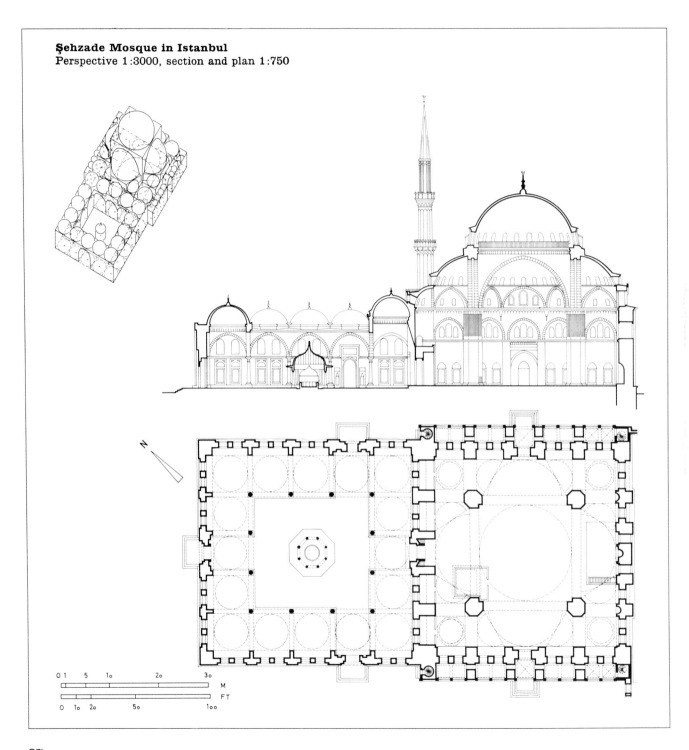

Şehzade Mosque in Istanbul
Perspective 1:3000, section and plan 1:750

0 1   5   1o   2o   3o
                                    M
                                    FT
0   1o   2o   5o   1oo

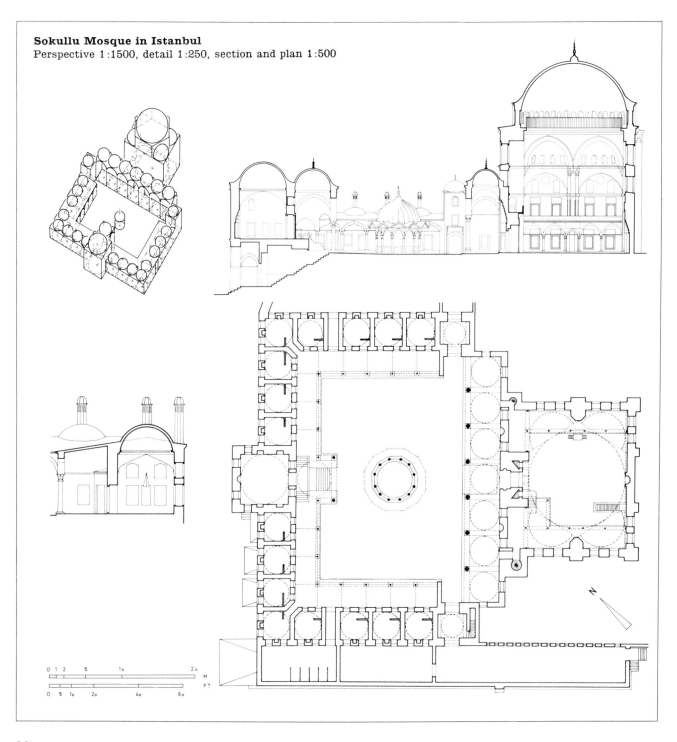

Sokullu Mosque in Istanbul
Perspective 1:1500, detail 1:250, section and plan 1:500

0 1 2   5   1o   2o
                                      M
                                      FT
0   5 1o   2o   4o   6o

2. The Mosque

The Development of the Early Ottoman Style in Bursa

Two ground plans are distinguishable in the early mosques of Bursa:

(1) The vaulted pier type which became the fundamental design for the citizens' mosques. One of the first examples of this type is the Ulu-Cami at Bursa.

(2) The ⊥-shaped type, which usually consisted of two square domes with an upper storey. Both domes had at each side two tower rooms which were used as studios.

The piered mosque is based on ancient Islamic tradition, whereas the ⊥-shaped ground plan appeared for the first time in early Ottoman architecture. The early versions of the former, found in North Africa, had serried ranks of piers and were often flat roofed. In the Ottoman Ulu-Cami, however, we find a limited number of cross-axes, each of them roofed with a dome or vault. The piered mosque was being gradually abandoned.

The ⊥-shaped ground plan was the basic structure from which was to stem all development of the uses of space in Turkish mosques. The oldest mosque of this kind was the Nitüfer-Hatun-Imareti in Iznik (Nikea) donated by Orhan's wife, the mother of Murad I. The Sultan's mosques in Bursa all exhibit, with minor variations, this type of ground plan.

A two-storeyed façade with an entrance-hall was another characteristic feature of the early mosques in Bursa (the Yeschil-Cami, the mosque of Mohamed I, is the only mosque to lack the front hall). On the right and left sides of the entrance were a storeroom and a staircase leading to the upper storey, where the Sultan's personal box was to be found. The arcaded front hall was designed for the use of latecomers to the service. In the front hall of the Beyazid Mosque the floor beside the arches is raised on either side of the entrance, and proof that these raised areas were meant for prayer is the existence of prayer niches on the walls.

The Beyazid Mosque in Bursa

The building of the Mosque of Beyazid, completed by the end of the fourteenth century, was frequently interrupted; it was then severely damaged by an earthquake in 1855. Most of the interior, together with the two domes, were almost completely destroyed. Restoration has drastically altered its original appearance and today only the front hall remains intact.

Hammer-Purgstall writes about the 'raw simplicity and melancholy' and the 'naked gray walls' of this mosque. It is no exaggeration to say that the front hall reveals a sudden new style of architecture, a new approach to the use of stone that cannot be compared with previous Islamic or medieval Christian styles. I say 'sudden' because there are hardly any signs of transitional stages. We know that buildings of the period of Orhan and his son, Murad (whose mosque-medrese is in the Bursa suburb of Cekirge), must have been influenced by Byzantine or Western styles, since they reveal no similarity with Beyazid's building, and it is even more surprising that this new style was at once so classically mature.

What is actually new in these Seljukian buildings is the idea of making the entrance a symmetrical and vaulted hall, thereby lessening its overbearing and massive impression. The principal façades of the buildings consist of almost nothing more than the portal itself, as is testified by the façades of the Kara-Tay Medrese and the Indscha Ninare at Konya, or the Cifte-Ninare at Siras. Also noteworthy is the restrained style of decoration, particularly in

▲ The Yildirim-Beyazid Mosque in Bursa: façade (after B. Ünsal)

comparison with that of mediaeval buildings of Asia Minor. For the first time in Islamic architecture we find emphasis on the beauty of the building material itself – gray, finely grained lime-stone – and on the exactness of its construction. The Beyazid Mosque impresses one not only by its simplicity, but also by the fine precision of its proportions. Clearly there has been a fundamental break with early Islamic tradition – perhaps it is an Islamic 'renaissance?' If we concentrate on one basic stylistic change, as occurred in Europe at the turn of the fourteenth century, we may be able to provide a positive answer. Yet we cannot really equate the entrance arcades of the early Florentine renaissance with the entrance halls of Beyazid. The starting point of the Italian renaissance was its conflict with antiquity, and this problem did not

90

confront the architect of the Beyazid Mosque. The fundamental task of renaissance architecture lay in the construction of a building to form a whole from independently functioning elements – column, arch and beam. Although here in Bursa as in Florence, a wonderful calmness emanates from the harmony of the whole, there is nonetheless a difference in apparently similar characteristics. The portico in Bursa is not formed from independently operating elements, but is rather carved out of a single massive block of stone; the façade does not appear to have been built of stone, but seems rather to have been turned into stone. Instead of a balance of stresses, of vertical and horizontal thrusts, a calmness reigns here, born not of harmony, but of the absolute.

The Yeschil-Cami (The 'Green' Mosque) in Bursa

The same kind of absolute calmness can be found in the interior of the Yeschil-Cami, one of the most beautiful examples of early Ottoman architecture. Its frescoes are incredibly varied; and the Külliye owes its name, Yeschil ('Green' in Turkish), to the blue-green tiles of the mausoleum and the interior of the mosque. The interior is completely enclosed, an independent structure which envelops the visitor in a cool crystal-like atmosphere, in which all sense of direction or movement is lost.

Closer examination of the shell reveals affinities with the vaulted hall of the Beyazid Mosque. Its harmony does not spring from the balance of opposing stresses, but from the structure of the shell itself. The interior appears to have been hollowed out of a single block of stone. The walls are in no way separate planes, hence there is no impression of a structure built up according to laws of support and stress.

A comparison with early-renaissance architecture in Italy clarifies the characteristics of this architectural style. Let us consider the buildings of Brunelleschi in Florence; his pillars, arches and framework stand out from the white walls because of their dark color. They emphasize the harmony and dynamics, accentuate the tectonic form and make us aware of the play of weight in the design.

The Yeschil-Cami, on the contrary, does not reveal a tectonic method and does not have resort to the same means. Characteristic of this building are the 'stalactites' which form a transition between the vertical and horizontal planes. Originally such 'stalactites' are thought to have been used in the construction of old wooden buildings, but although this may be so, one still wonders why this natural phenomenon should have become so characteristic of Ottoman stone architecture – not only characteristic but indeed basic to the structure. Stalactite forms were most often used at critical points of support – such as columns, domes or walls. In the Yeschil-Cami the transition from walls to dome – from a square plan to a circular base – is made by a tambour consisting of stalactite forms. The buttresses of the large arch between the two principal rooms rest on corbels, which again consist of stalactites.

The stalactite is used at the point where weight calls the greatest support, and gives the impression of frozen suspension. The stone thus has two images; one of crystalline hardness and rigidity, the other of weightlessness. The stone is carved and polished from top to bottom, from front to back, hollowed out layer by layer.

The stalactite is a petrified substance, formed by the action of continuously trickling water – by thus 'freezing,' it is freed from the laws of gravity. How can one understand the relation between pillar and weight, if all relations consist of these frozen and suspended forms? We recognize here an attempt to escape and transcend the laws of gravity. Moreover, the attempt uses a structure outside tectonic forms; a structure subjected to a geometrical law – similar to the crystal-formation in nature – and which works independently of gravity.

The stalactites' brackets, the downward-thrusting stalactites of the cupola and the tambour, as we find them in the Yeschil-Cami, become weight and latent power personified. By means of this frozen effect, the stone loses its weight, yet is simultaneously transformed into a crystal-like form. The prismatic bodies which form the tambour also give the same effect: the area of transition between the cupola and the walls is neutralized as to its lines of direction. The rhombic areas neutralize the contrast between the horizontal and vertical; by pointing simultaneously in both directions, the facets seem to make the cupola weightless.

The Period of the Conquest of Byzantium

After the conquest of Constantinople, the Turkish architects were faced with a new and major problem: to redevelop this capital as an Islamic city as quickly as possible. Constantinople had been the focal point of the Eastern Church for more than a thousand years. Its founders and leaders had maintained the image of the heavenly Jerusalem for centuries. The aim of the new inhabitants was now to dispense with ancient tradition and to give the capital an Islamic character. Confronted with the Justinian Church of St. Sophia, the victors' artistic consciousness was aroused and so began their attempts to surpass the grandeur and splendor of the ancient church.

The Turks did not, however, destroy the building, but transformed it into a mosque and subse-

quently took great care of it. They continued to consider this beautiful monument as a standard by which to measure their own creations. On this point, literature dealing with Turkish architecture is divided into two groups; one group, consisting mainly of western authorities, believes Turkish architecture to be derived exclusively from Byzantine, and denies it any originality,

▼ St. Sophia: Section and plan (after C. Gureitt)

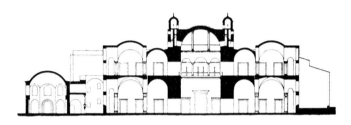

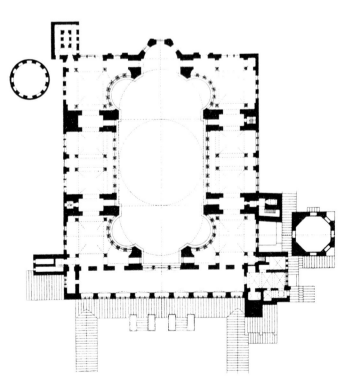

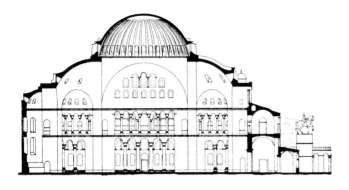

▲ St. Sophia : Cross section (after C. Gureitt)

(Byzantine) sources and traditions.

Using as examples the Beyazid Mosque and the Yeschil-Cami, I have tried to show how Turkish architecture departed from the Seljuk tradition. In order to trace its development in Constantinople, we shall first consider briefly what buildings were in fact responsible for the new directions taken. Writing about Turkish mosques in 1953, I described St. Sophia as follows :

'How could Turkish architects understand the earlier Christian-Byzantine architecture from their point of view? . . . Contrary to their own use of space with its characteristics of crystal effects and bright interiors, the latter had created the open, delicate, unfettered interior of St. Sophia. Here were fluid forms merging into one another, hazy outlines, an undefined shell. Byzantine and Turkish architecture have but one thing in common : their ability to give an impression of weightlessness. This, however, was achieved in completely different ways. A closer examination of the St. Sophia's structure will show that the tectonic form was not continued (as in Turkish architecture) but consciously avoided. Everything in the interior that might seem solid is disguised – even the gentlest outline is obliterated. We recognize the corner pillars, the true supports of the dome, only by their outer edges. Even the principal vaults are mere outlines. All connections and transitions are lightly sketched lines or points, lost to view in the shimmering gold expanse of wall. The body of the building becomes a matter of planes, the interplay of single lines and points. Instead of being obviously supported by pillars, the dome seems suspended in air, and from the dome, all forms merge outwards into one another. Each part is connected with the dome and dependent on it. What is the significance of this 'suspension' in an architectural system? It is freedom from gravity. The solid body is bound by gravity

while the other group, mostly nationalistic Turkish authorities, attempts to refute Byzantine or any other influences. The first group overlooks the fact that the buildings which span the development from Bursa to the Beyazid-Külliye in Edirne are wholly independent achievements. It also overlooks the fact that a sense of competition could only arise since the victors were already equipped to take over the achievements of those whom they had conquered. As for the second group, their postulations are historically untenable, for nowhere in the history of any art is there a style that has suddenly flowered without drawing on earlier styles. Turkish architecture definitely underwent major changes after the conquest of Constantinople, and the formal influence of St. Sophia becomes obvious when we consider the Constantinople era as a whole. One would not, however, be justified in remarking that this fruitful Byzantine influence merely produced enthusiastic imitations; in its highest form it resulted in creative transformation.

In this way, St. Sophia was definitely a stimulus for Turkish architects during the fifteenth and sixteenth centuries. Yet it was never a 'model' in the accepted sense of the world. Turkish architects, like all true artists, both created within their own tradition and drew from foreign to the earth and is dependent on its laws. Suspension and buoyancy, however, imply the reversal of tectonic forms. One can only talk of tectonic forms if the body rests on the ground.

'In St. Sophia, however, the whole structure seems to swing from above, like a weightless bell, to brush the ground without being tectonic-

▼ St. Sophia: Interior (after an engraving by G. Fossati)

ally linked to it. The ground is no longer the base of structure, merely another plane. Hence the shell of the interior seems to open into endless expanses, rather than being a precise sum-area of the building's walls. As long as any plane appears as the surface area of given structure, it has comprehensible mathematically calculable proportions. In this case, however, its relation to the total structure is completely disguised and therefore loses its said proportions. Its dimensions melt into indefinable expanses. In St. Sophia, the whole system seems to float above us in space; the great hall seems to stretch in all directions, into infinity. The longer we remain in the hall, the more things seem to float around us. In experiencing these endless dimensions we become steeped in an illusion of eternity.'

Clearly, therefore, the Byzantines considered space very differently from the Turks. The former pursued the idea of infinity, which they attempted to create by their hovering, weightless dome. The interior of an early Ottoman mosque, however, resembled a crystalline entity. In both cases, there is an attempt to go beyond gravity; the respective architects search for formal laws over and above those demanded by gravity. Their attempts are, however, very different. What impressed the Turkish architects in St. Sophia? It was not the idea of the 'floating firmament' but St. Sophia's basic method of construction, particularly that of the dome.

Only some fifty years later did the influence of St. Sophia on other architecture make itself felt. The first great Turkish building erected in Istanbul was the Mosque of Beyazid II, whose ground plan is similar to that of St. Sophia.

During their first year of occupation, the Turks erected two small mosques, the Mahmut Pasha and Murad Pasha, that have the ⊥-

shaped ground plan. The Mohamed II Mosque and the Atik-Ali Mosque have a new ground plan. They no longer have a square Mihrab room vaulted with domes. The Mihrab now has the shape of a halved square and is vaulted with a half-dome. So for the first time we see an attempt to combine the dome and the half-dome in one building. Because of this, pendentives were used as a means of transition from a square base to the circle, and the position of the central room is more strongly emphasized. No longer do we see two rooms of equal importance, as in the Bursa mosques. Now we have a domed hall with an adjoining Mihrab room. A further development is the disappearance of the walls that separate the lateral rooms from the central hall. Like the aisles of Renaissance churches, the adjoining roooms now become domed quadrants with vaulted cross-beams.

The mosques of Mahmut Pasha and Murad Pasha in Istanbul do not equal the artistry of either the Beyazid Mosque or the Yeschil-Cami in Bursa. In the latter, attempts to combine the dome with the half-dome were only partially successful. How this particular problem was dealt with in the Mosque of Mohamed II cannot be ascertained since the mosque was completely destroyed by an earthquake in the eighteenth century. However, the Mosque of Atik-Ali Pasha built some forty years after the Mohamed II Mosque, contains clumsy pendentives, inconclusive cornices and top-heavy proportions.

The Beyazid Mosque in Istanbul

The Mosque of Beyazid II, designed by Hayreddin, is the first building in which new achievements within an independent tradition can be seen. In its use of space, the mosque is very similar to the Church of St. Sophia. The dome is supported by two half-domes and two arches. The pendentives connect the dome with the walls.

If one compares this design with that of St. Sophia, it appears that similar forms have produced different space-effects. The fusing of spherical forms which had been so easily achieved in St. Sophia by doing away with clear outlines, are altogether avoided in the Beyazid Mosque. In St. Sophia there is a single transition from the large arch to the half-dome. No outline points clearly to the principal supporting arch. In the Beyazid Mosque, however, massive arches hinder the effect of effortless suspension. The half-dome is, moreover, slightly raised by a concealed tambour. The dome of St. Sophia is a pure hemisphere, and viewed from beneath, it seems even more as though it were about to open at its outer edges. Compared with the Beyazid dome it appears complete and self-contained. A further essential difference between the two interiors is the way in which the aisles supplement the central hall. The aisles, galleries and adjoining rooms of St. Sophia form a darker surround to the bright central hall. Between lightly

▼ The Beyazid II Mosque in Bursa (after C. Gureitt)

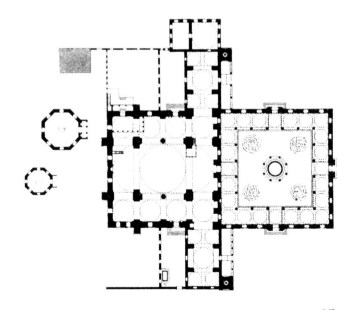

95

polished columns and capitals, these rooms seem to stretch away to infinity. The limits of the Beyazid rooms, however, are clearly visible, and supplement the central hall. The general effect, therefore, is that of an undivided interior, a solid, unmoving mass. The architect of the Beyazid Mosque stresses outlines. The emphasis on the solidity of a single element of building is not tectonic; and here, Hayreddin remains faithful to the new style begun in Bursa. Pillars, arches, pendentives and the small lateral arches seem to have been fused.

An examination of Sinan's mosques will show us that Beyazid is still in the early stages of stylistic conflicts, and is therefore not altogether divorced from stylistic conflicts. Hayreddin's genius is evident wherever he creates within his own tradition, in the Beyazid Külliye in Edirne, and in the courtyard of the Beyazid Mosque in Istanbul. Indeed, the style here of his windows and portals later became an established pattern.

The Beyazid Mosque in Edirne

Stylistic differences even occur in mosques where earlier interior characteristics have not changed. Such is the mosque with a single interior, whose primary form consisted of a cube and hemisphere. This type of mosque was, apart from the vaulted pier mosque, the earliest type of Ottoman mosque. The oldest extant specimen is the Yeschil-Cami in Isnik, built in 1392, but it was adopted again in early Istanbul buildings and smaller mosques donated by statesmen or wealthy citizens. It was first employed in a Sultan's mosque in the Beyazid Külliye at Edirne, and again forty years later in the Selimiye, which Süleyman built in memory of his father, Selim. This mosque has been attributed to Hayreddin, but if we compare it with his earlier building in Edirne, it reveals uncertainties of style not apparent there. Both

the exterior and the interior of the Beyazid Külliye are perfectly simple. There are no superfluous structures that might detract from the cube, and light from uniformly set windows increases the effect of absolute serenity in the interior.

We find in the Selimiye Mosque several new forms: buttresses on outer walls, an externally constructed dome tambour with a flying buttress on its corners, and a form of frieze decorating the outer ledge. At first sight these innovations might seem to imply a new structural form. But a more thorough examination shows that in fact the structure did not result from any weight and support ratio. In any case, it is not convincing in the structural sense, and only serves to enrich the exterior. The simple, beautiful tranquility of the Beyazid Mosque is disturbed by the presence of these ornamentations – innovation, here, has not been successful.

Sinan

Early Life

Sinan's birth date and origins cannot be established with certainty. Contemporary reports and documents are contradictory. According to these he is thought to have lived for anything from 95 to 140 years (these are, however, Islamic years which follow the lunar cycle and are consequently eleven days shorter than the Christian year). He is believed to have come from Albania or Serbia, although Austria and Central Anatolia are also mentioned. Ernst Egli has examined all these references and, having compared various reports and converted the Islamic lunar year into the Christian solar year, he concludes that 1491 is a likely date for Sinan's birth.

It is even more difficult to establish the

architect's origins. Most probably Sinan came to Istanbul as a Dervish and was later enlisted in the Janissaries. A friend of Sinan, the poet Mustafa Saî, mentioned the architect in his 'Architectural Wonders.' 'The esteemed servant Sinan, son of Abdulmenan, the famous architect-in-chief who himself as a son of Abdullah (i.e. a non-Moslem) came to the palace in his earlier years, according to the blessed Ottoman custom, together with Greek Dervish youths from the Vilayet province of Karaman and its towns; he was taken into service for some time and was then apprenticed to the Persian army, where he reached the rank of Janissary.'

Other reports agree that Sinan spent his childhood in Kayseri. Whether, however, he was born there or whether his family came as refugees from the west to Istanbul and thence to Central Anatolia, remains a mystery.

From Sinan's autobiography, we learn that he joined the campaigns to Rhodes and Belgrade as a Janissary and later the campaign to Mohacz as a hussar. 'Then I was made a Yayabasi (infantry captain) and later Zenberek-basi (Chief Mechanic) and joined the campaign to Belgrade (1534). On my return I became captain of the bodyguard and accompanied the Sultan on the campaign to Corfu and Balia (1537) and to Kara Bogdan.' If we accept 1491 as the year of his birth, it means that Sinan was aged 50 when he began his career as an architect. In 1539 he was made chief of the Empire's corps of architects. Because of his earlier rank as mechanic, crafts-man and engineer, Sinan had gained much experience in military projects – castles, fortifications and bridges. His campaigns had also given him first-hand knowledge of architecture in the Balkans and other Islamic countries. Mustafa Saî reports that Sinan created 334 buildings, and when his first big mosque in Istanbul, the Şehzade Mosque, was completed, he was already fifty years old.

Sinan's First Major Work

The first major building which we may attribute with certainty to Sinan was not, in fact, located in Istanbul. Husrev Pasha, then governor of Syria, employed him to build a Külliye in Aleppo. At the time Sinan was campaigning in Persia. This consisted of a single mosque, similar to the Selimiye Mosque in Istanbul, and was flanked by a medrese, a bath-house and two other dependent buildings. In his design Sinan retained the established ground plan of a vaulted square interior with a forecourt. Sinan's new methods of organization which we have noted in his masterpiece, the Süleyman unit, are already clear here : a symmetrical arrangement of the whole is contrasted with asymmetrically planned paths. Sinan laid out the paths that lead from the Külliye's main entrances to the mosque in such a way that the observer is never conscious of the axes that underlie the whole.

The Şehzade Mosque in Istanbul

With this building, Sinan begins his break with Byzantine architecture. Hayreddin's Beyazid Mosque was the first attempt to break away from Byzantine tradition ; forty years later Sinan encountered problems that his predecessor had only touched on. Yet Hayreddin's work enabled Sinan to ascertain how far Byzantine styles could be adapted. In each of the three large mosques which Sinan built over the next fifteen years, he used variations on the scheme of St. Sophia.

In the Şehzade Mosque, the symmetrical axes which form the Church of St. Sophia are translated into a form consisting of symmetrical points related to a center. Some twelve years later, Sinan became even more daring : in the Mihrimah Mosque the half-dome is abandoned and the dome is supported by the arcaded walls. The mosque was donated by Princess Mihrimah, daughter of Süleyman and Hurrem, and can be dated between 1540 and 1555. It was, therefore, either completed three years before, or twelve years after, the Şehzade Mosque. Its stylistic maturity, however, suggests the latter date. Another of Sinan's works, built for Sal-Mahmud Pasha in the suburbs of Eyüb, confirms this. In this earlier building (by almost four years) – its cubic style is strongly reminiscent of early Ottoman buildings – Sinan tried for the first time to support the dome directly on the arcaded exterior walls. This building could therefore be considered as an intermediate step, where Sinan is still experimenting with his new forms. But in the Süleyman Mosque, where Sinan intended to surpass St. Sophia in both dimensions and artistry, he reverted to the half-dome system.

In the first of these three buildings, the Şehzade Mosque, Sinan had already been successful in transforming the stylistic character of early Ottoman architecture. Here, the architect adapts Byzantine formal elements to his own ends. The structure of stone is used in a new way: the finished structure is achieved by reducing the whole to single components.

To make this clear, I should like first to compare a Renaissance building with a similar plan to the Şehzade Mosque. A suitable example is the Church of Santa Maria della Consolazione in Todi, whose trefoil-shaped ground plan can be traced, although in a roundabout way, to Byzantine ground plans. Like other Renaissance buildings, the interior consists of elements whose functions are immediately apparent. The interior is bounded by pilasters, beams and white walls between. Pilasters and beams are structural components and give the whole its shape and proportion, and the geometrical shape is thus dependent on its various elements. The system of pilaster and beam extends along the walls and the dome. In the Şehzade Mosque we encounter a completely different structural system. Anyone acquainted with Greek or Renaissance architecture would look in vain for, as it were, 'self-contained' buildings. The dome of Sinan's building forms the starting-point of the whole structure. From here the arches and smaller half-domes radiate outwards. The various components extend from the top to the bottom. They all form such a closely knit unit that it is impossible to distinguish at first sight just where, in this complex of spherical shells, the stress lies; whether the dome is supported by the arches and the latter by the pillars, or whether the dome itself supports everything. Certainly the spans are not immediately apparent. In a Renaissance building the dome is always the terminus, a comprehensive 'answer' to pillars and walls. Conversely, in Sinan's buildings, the dome is the 'beginning:' it is responsible for the structure of the whole.

This kind of structure is based on the principle of stone-cutting or crystal-polishing. This is a 'deductive' process and contrasts with Renaissance structure, where a number of single components are used to build the whole. A deductive process in the structure of stone architecture does not necessarily call for clear distinctions between what is supported and its elements of support. What we must accept is the concept of a single huge block of stone. Only in this way can we conceive of smaller forms obtained from larger ones; a development from the top to the bottom. This is seen particularly in the style of the central pillars. These are separated into two parts: the uppermost part is fluted while the lower part consists of an octagonal prism with smooth surfaces and hard edges. But only the prismatic of the pillar stands free. Towards the external walls the fluted part marges into the side arches, which in turn merge into the external walls. These pillars, side arches and external walls together form an indissoluble unit. Sinan also tries to reduce the area between pillars and the effect of weight by stalactites.

The use of stalactites between the walls and domes continues around the pillars, and serves as a further connection between pillars and walls. The fluting on the upper part of the pillars draws attention to the downward bearing stress of the dome. It is just this part which complies with that of the intermediate part of the external walls onto which the side arches join and connect with the main pillars. The spandrels between the arch and the external walls are filled with stalactites, and consequently the arches appear to have no downward thrust. We conclude that the weight of the vault is, therefore, supported at the same points as the stalactite spandrels, the fluted parts of the pillars and the small arcaded arch on the external wall.

As in early schemes, the ground plan of the mosque remains a square. The original cuboid form was preserved here too, although not in each room, but as an imaginary cube, enclosing the whole mosque. The height of the room is equal to the side of the square in the original form. Thus, within the cube of the ancient Turkish mosque we now find a many sided polished prism.

The Mihrimah Mosque

The Mihrimah Mosque was the next major building in which Sinan attempted to solve the same problems, but from another angle. He had used four half-domes in the Şehzade Mosque, but here he does away with them altogether. Four narrow, arcaded walls, interrupted by windows, and four spherical spandrels effect the transition from the cube-like central hall to the dome. Sinan also restricts the use of old Turkish elements – stalactites, for example, are confined wholly to the pillar capitals. In this building he attempted to improve on Byzantine structures (arcaded walls and pendentives). The walls in the Mihrimah Mosque appear very distinct when compared with those in the Şehzade

Mosque. Hard, sharply defined edges stress the various areas and transitional points. Also strongly reminiscent of St. Sophia is the way in which corners are treated – the vaulted corner arches have no visible means of support. Yet the artistic effect of these analogous treatments of the corner is not the same. The shell of the Mihrimah Mosque does not appear to float like a 'weightless bell.' On closer observation we realize that Sinan has used the same principle of structure as in the Şehzade Mosque. There is no differentiation between vault, pilaster and walls. The spandrels and arches do not differ from one another; the surface of the vaults merges immediately into the shape of the dome. If we were to imagine that all those parts which fill in the shell were removed, the remaining arches and walls beneath would not form a skeleton that would stand up on its own. No single part of the system of walls could be subtracted – all the parts must be there for the building to have any unity.

The close-knit nature of this shell excludes any illusion of movement and expanse. The equal distribution of light to all parts of the building also contributes to the clear, compact effect of the structure as a whole.

The Süleyman Mosque in Istanbul

This is one of the most important buildings in Turkish architecture. Here Sinan set out to prove to the world that he could surpass the Greeks. The building of this mosque was a turning point in his career. Surprisingly enough he adopted in principle the ground plan of St. Sophia – surprising, since he also intended to surpass this Church. Why then did he choose an identical ground plan?

The sequence of the Şehzade-Mihrimah-Süleyman mosques seems to have been intentional. Sinan experimented with two schemes opposed to that of St. Sophia – first using four half-domes (Şehzade) and then doing away with them (Mihrimah). The Süleyman Mosque was the last building in which the original St. Sophia ground scheme plays a decisive role. After this, Sinan abandoned this scheme. With the sole exception of the Kiliç Ali Mosque in Istanbul, we no longer find the combination of dome and half-dome, in which the latter are of the same radius as the central dome. This is one of Sinan's last works, completed in 1580, and does not, therefore, belong to the period between the Süleyman and the Selim Mosque (Edirne).

We must therefore suppose that in the Süleyman Mosque Sinan embarked on a final struggle to solve the formal problems of Byzantine architecture, and at the same time free himself from its patterns. So the idea of surpassing an existing building by making use of its own scheme is not so strange.

Compared with other works by Sinan, the Süleyman Mosque is the only building in which constructional elements are noticeable. The interior occasionally resembles Roman interiors. Yet the detached corner pillars as well as the corbel-moulding between the walls and the vaults, although stressing the construction, do not have the effect of Roman interiors. Like the Şehzade and Mihrimah, space in the Süleyman Mosque has gained its form through the principle of compensatory structure, but despite its formal agreement with Roman and Byzantine styles, it preserves its own character.

Replacing continuity of spherical forms (as in St. Sophia) we find in the Süleyman Mosque constant changes between spherical and level areas as well as between half-domes and arcaded walls. The spherical forms of St. Sophia merge softly into one another. Sinan stresses the difference between level and spherical area, and does away with effects of downward stress. Sinan has also used pointed arches as a means of checking the image of this stress.

Sinan's ground plan retains right angles and straight lines. He therefore did not insert the apses of the St. Sophia ground plan. The strict square formed by the walls on the ground floor serve to remind us of the original cube of which the shell seems to have been hewn.

A noteworthy detail is the use of stalactite-spandrels in the corners. Plain, spherical spandrels would not have sufficiently stressed the contrast between horizontal and vaulted areas, and, undefinable in darker corners, they would have detracted from the solid shape of the interior. By fitting the spandrels with stalactites, Sinan prevented the interior from disappearing, as it were, into space.

The architect intentionally avoided innovation in the form of this building, and one of the results was the crystal clear structure of the stone.

These variations on an axial ground plan, using the possibilities of a central symmetry, present an isolated case in the history of architecture. Sinan's adaptations of Byzantine architecture show that he was only concerned with its basic geometrical forms. He therefore used neither the technique nor the art of construction – but this should by no means imply that he was merely playing a masterly game with form. His later works show that he was chiefly concerned to crystallize all these variants in order to produce a perfect form for the interior of the mosque. The Süleyman Mosque marks the end of his relationship with Byzantine architecture ; he recognized in the latter a means of developing and establishing his own ideas.

In the following chapter, we see how Sinan dealt with the hexagonal or octagonal mosque, and hence with the problem of the central hall.

The Period after the Süleyman Mosque

The Rustem Pasha Mosque in Istanbul

Four years after the completion of the Süleyman Mosque (1560) Sinan began work on the Rustem Pasha Mosque, and here revealed a new style. The mosque was donated by the Vizier, Rustem Pasha, husband of Princess Mihrimah. The plan of the mosque is very similar to that of the Mihrimah Mosque: a square central interior with aisles, each of which consists of three cross-beamed vaults. However, these rooms differ considerably in their structure and especially in their relation to the dome. We find no half-domes of the same diameter as the central dome nor walls of equal size throughout. These Byzantine forms are no longer in evidence, and while the forms employed are not new, they are smaller and are part of a new method of construction.

The large spherical spandrels (see the Mihrimah and Süleyman mosques) are now replaced by smaller half-domes. The semi-circular bases of these domes are connected to the walls by means of Stalactites. Supporting walls fill the space between two such walls. The transition from the square to the dome is therefore achieved by an octagonal area, with walls supported by four more equally sized walls and half-domes. In this way we have a facetted transitional area. By replacing the pendentives with half-domes, Sinan achieves more consistency in the interior of the mosque.

As original Byzantine forms were abandoned, so other reminders also disappeared. Earlier Turkish elements, especially the stalactite, again begin to play an important role. Pillars merge into the background. Large, octagonal pillars, covered with tiles, already suggest the octagon from below. No capitals, but only a few stalactites on the corners are connected with the vaults. In this way, the sharp-cornered prismatic pillars appear so strongly merged that the openings of the vaults appear to have been hollowed out. The new method of the transition to the dome makes a lower height for the inter-

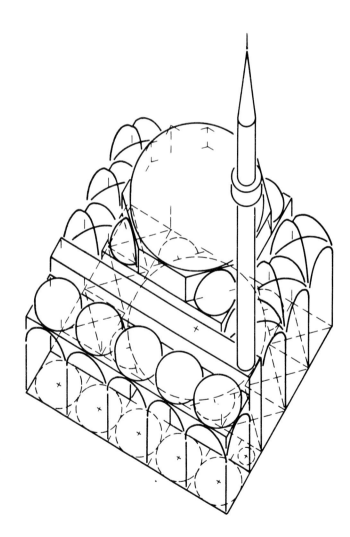

▲ The Rustem Pasha Mosque in Istanbul: Perspective

mediate zone possible. The half-domes at the corners connect the dome with the walls in a more rigid manner than the spherical spandrels. As the result of the effect of these details, the room gains a more solid and compact form.

The Sokullu Mosque

Apart from the octagon in the Rustem Pasha Mosque, another structure particularly occupied Sinan's mind : that of the single central dome supported on six pillars, each with two half-domes on either side as means of transition from the square to the circle. This type originated in the early Ottoman period, but was never employed in Istanbul The Uç Serefeli Mosque in Edirne (completed in 1447) is one of the most beautiful examples of its kind.

In this earlier spatial form, Sinan recognized further possibilities which would be useful in his new conception of interiors. Ten years after the completion of the Rustem Pasha Mosque, he transformed this old form with great technical skill into the mosque of the Vizier, Sokullu Mohamed Pasha. Two smaller mosques which Sinan had built at about the same time as the Süleyman, were prototypes.

The Mosque of Sinan Pasha was the first of the two prototype mosques. It was completed in 1554, two years after the death of its donator. The second mosque, Kara-Ahmet Pasha, has a more complicated history, because of the troubled political life experienced by its donator. It was completed several years after the completion of the Sokullu.

The interior of the Sinan Pasha appears to be a hall because of its high vaulting tangential to the dome, between the main room and the aisles. The interior of the Kara-Ahmet forms a more stringent unity. The room no longer has the distinct aisles, and only the two side walls are transformed into small, two-storeyed galleries.

In the Sokullu Mosque, Sinan did not differentiate between the main room and the aisles : as if captured by a thin glossy shell, this interior merges into a single body. Never before had Sinan achieved such unity and clarity. A comparison of this ground plan with those of previous hexagonal mosques reveals the origins of this new effect. In the Sinan Pasha Mosque, the aisles are separated from the central hall by means of cross-pillars and angled double arches. The transition from circle to square remains invisible. The small domes leading to the main dome are hidden behind the vaults, thus giving this room the true effect of a hall. In the Kara-Ahmet Mosque, the aisles are missing and the interior is not divided by cross-arches.

His use of half-domes to effect the transition from circle to square, which deepens the unity of the interior as a whole, brings Sinan one step closer to a solution of the problems inherent in the ground plan of the Sokullu Mosque. The interior of the Sokullu draws no distinction between the main hall and the aisles, although it is not strictly square. The half-domes extend up to the outer walls at the side. The central pillars on which they rest belong to the outer walls ; they are built out from these walls, but remain half-contained by them. The two side arcades appear to have been added, like the Mimber, as an afterthought : they have no relation to the interior shell, and do not form its boundaries. Because of the way in which the dome is built — square and rectangle merge — the difference between the square projections of the dome's tangents and the rectangular ground plan disappear in the interior seen as a whole. By building walls with centrally placed pillars, Sinan achieved a masterly merging of hexagon and square. The interior is a fusion of various geometrical forms — half-dome, hexagonal prism and rectangle — which underlines its compact unity. At the same time as this mosque was being built, Sinan's last great building, the mosque for his new master, Selim II, was being erected in Edirne.

The Selim Mosque in Edirne

This mosque was Sinan's most mature creation. His usual cycle of creative imagination was to evolve bold theories, put them into practice and then stand back in objective critical analysis. Sinan here put his now fully tested discoveries into practice, and the result was a masterpiece of Turkish architecture. The Rustem Pasha and the Sokullu mosques were smaller buildings, lacking the scale of those of the Sultans, so important to Sinan. He chose an octagonal ground plan, already tried out in the Rustem Pasha. A comparison with the latter shows that the path traced from the Rustem Pasha to the Selim mosques runs parallel to that between the Sinan Pasha and the Sokullu mosques. He used the aisled design of the Rustem Pasha in his new mosque; at ground-storey level the central hall was separated from the side rooms by high pillars and arches. By not building aisles in the Sokullu Mosque he had achieved an effect of a shell carved from a single block. In the Selim Mosque he achieved the same, using an octagonal ground-plan. This octagonal shape allowed him to create a symmetrical form radiating from the center – hence the effects of serene immobility and the crystalline formation of the interior.

Both these qualities, basic to all Turkish architecture, were brought to a peak of perfection by Sinan. In this mosque, Sinan's use of the octagon achieved perfect harmony. A circle of alternating supporting walls and half-domes transfers the weight of the dome to eight powerful pillars. This circle is echoed by another one beneath it, comprising a series of large arches which reverses the rhythmical order of the upper

one. In this mosque the transition from rectangle to circle is expertly managed, bringing the original cuboid form and the dome into a harmonious relationship. Pillars and arches stand out in relief against the walls, defining the interior shell without becoming obtrusive.

Sinan's autobiography reveals that the Church of St. Sophia remained his touchstone of artistic achievement throughout his career. In connecttion with the Selim Mosque, he wrote : 'Architects in Christian countries may rank themselves above Mohammedans in technical skill, owing to the failure of the latter to achieve anything approaching the dome of St. Sophia. This assertion of insurmountable difficulty has wounded the author of these writings. However, with God's help and the Sultan's mercy. I have succeeded in building a dome for Sultan Selim's mosque which is four ells greater in diameter and six ells higher than that of the St. Sophia.'

Sinan continued to be active after the building of this mosque, although not all the designs from which he worked can be assumed to have been his own. There are no further developments in the shaping of mosque interiors, except for a new design of cincture for the half-dome. This new style is evident in the Azapkapisi, the Eski-Valide, the Mesih Pasha and the Nischanci-Mohamed Pasha mosques. This emphasis on the half-dome disrupts the harmony of the transition from supporting walls to half-dome, blurring the sense of hard tension between flat and hollowed planes.

Only two mosques, most probably designed by Sinan himself, deviate from this type, namely the Piyale Pasha Mosque (1573), and the Kilic-Ali Mosque (1580). The latter reproduces the ground plan of the Süleyman Mosque on a smaller scale. For the Piyale Pasha Mosque, strangely enough, Sinan reverts to one of the oldest Ottoman designs, the pillared hall of the Ulu-Cami.

Because this mosque seems an anachronism in the course of Sinan's development, it has often not been acknowledged as one of his buildings. But it is hardly likely that this mosque should have been the work of a younger man seeking to surpass Sinan's school by deliberately reverting to archaic styles. Had this been the case, this style should, logically, have been developed, but there is subsequently no trace of a similar building or of its influencing contemporary styles.

If we think back to the Sinan Pasha Mosque and its apparently anachronistic relation to the Süleyman and the Mihrimah mosques, we can draw a parallel between it and the Piyale Pasha mosque. Both were built at the end of a certain phase of Sinan's development : the first, at the time of the Süleyman Mosque, when Sinan was freeing himself from Byzantine influence, the second, in 1573, after the completion of the Selim Mosque which marked Sinan's full maturity. In both cases, therefore, the mosques marked a terminal point in experiment. Having avoided routine all his life, Sinan twice reverted to old designs to escape repetition and stagnation. The first time he was seeking to create something new out of old forms ; the second time he was probably acting in a spirit of resignation – he was now aged over eighty. He was fortunate to live long enough to witness the completion of his plans, something which escaped many other great master-builders. The tragedy of the dome of St. Peter's in Rome, whose history can be traced from the elder Sangallo to Bernini, from 1410 to 1657, shows what could happen when a project was left without a master mind.

Plates

Istanbul

109 **The Mihrimah Mosque.** View of the Mihrab side (south-east façade).

110 General view of the mosque and the adjoining Medrese, seen from the north. By grouping the Medrese cells around the mosque courtyard, Sinan has changed the Medrese into an integral part of the mosque.

111 View of the forecourt from the north-west.

112 The small cemetery garden at the northern entrance to the mosque.

113 View of the Mihrab wall from the main entrance.

114–15 Interior of the mosque. View looking towards the north-west wall. Widespread damage in the nineteenth century caused by an earthquake necessitated almost complete restoration.

116 View of the interior from the north-west. The painting on the walls and vaults is more recent.

117 One of the four pendentives which effect the transition from the rectangular ground plan to the dome.

118 Arch and gallery above the main entrance.

Edirne

119 **The Selim Mosque.** General view of the south-east façade. The Külliye buildings have a similar design to those of the Süleyman Mosque: forecourt, mosque and burial garden, surrounded by the medrese, sanatorium and bazaar.
This is the last of the mosques Sinan built for Sultans. The minarets at the four corners of the square are 259 feet high – the highest of all Ottoman minarets, and also the most delicate in all Islamic architecture.

120 Dome and system of supports in the Selim Mosque. The dome is 96 feet across.

121 South-west entrance to the Mosque, and south-west façade of the forecourt.

122 Base of the corner pillar at the main entrance to the mosque.

123 Forecourt.

124 Main door, viewed from the forecourt. The well in the middle of the forecourt provides water for the ritual washing which must take place before one may enter the mosque.

125 Main dome and the system of stresses, seen from above.

126 Interior. The aisles between the pillars and outer walls are scarcely visible.

127 Detail of the pulpit in the middle of the mosque. (A small spiral staircase is built into the pillar.)

128 In the upper part of the building, outer walls and main pillars literally grow together.

129 View towards the north-east wall.

130 View between the pillars and the side wall.

131 Mimber.

132 Detail of a stalactite from the main door.

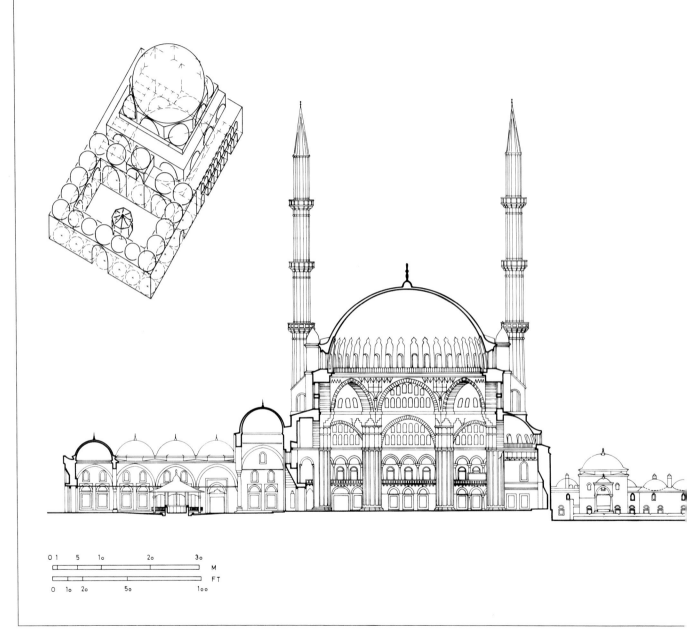

Selim Mosque in Edirne
Perspective 1:2000, longitudinal section 1:750 and plan 1:1200

O 1 5 1o   2o   3o
M
FT
O 1o 2o   5o   1oo

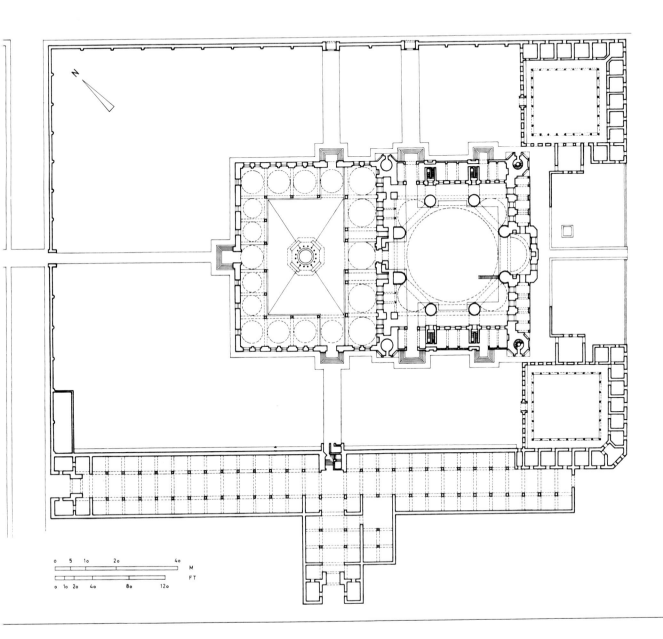

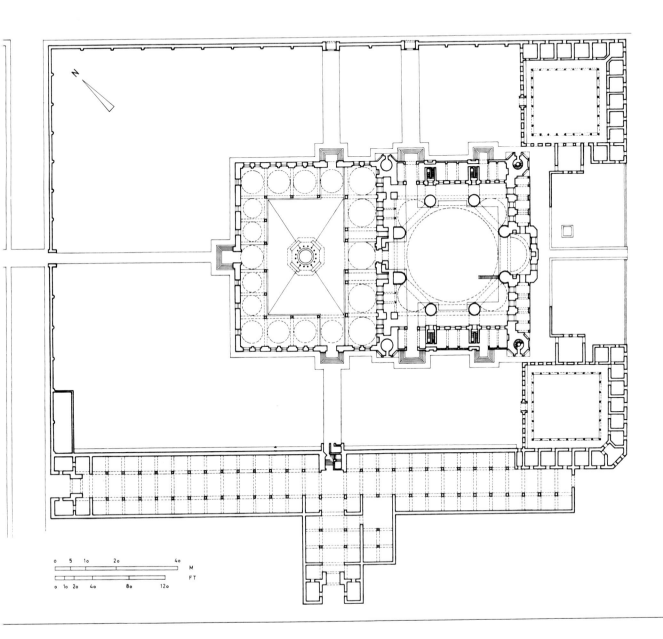

```
o  5  1o    2o        4o   M
                           F T
o  1o  2o  4o    8o    12o
```

Notes

Istanbul

The Mihrimah Mosque There is disagreement as to the dating of the Mihrimah Mosque. Estimates range from 1540-1555. Princess Mihrimah was a daughter of Süleyman and Hasseki-Hurem. In 1539 she married Rustem Pasha, later Grand Vizier. She died in 1558. Ernst Egli inclines to an early dating of the mosque, seeing a connection between the Princess's marriage and her donating the mosque, although he does not exclude the possibility of the building having been erected in the 1550's. A later date for the mosque seems the more likely, because its style, if compared to the Princes' Mosque of 1543, shows a development of style which brings it closer to the Süleyman Mosque. This hypothesis is supported by another building which we know to have been built in 1551: namely Zal Mahmut Pasha's mosque on the Golden Horn. In this building, with its reminders of the early Ottoman style, Sinan tried, obviously for the first time, to support the dome on the external walls. Since this mosque can scarcely have been built after the Mihrimah Mosque, we may be sure that the latter was not started at the time of Mihrimah's marriage, but some years before her death.

In the nineteenth century, the building was seriously damaged by an earthquake which destroyed the upper part of the minaret.

shops on either side. This was destroyed in the Russian war, and was not restored when the medreses and schools were rebuilt to form a museum.

Edirne

The Selim Mosque was built between 1569-1575, during the reign of Selim II, Süleyman's son. This mosque was one of the results of Sinan's many searches for form. Sinan here adopted the octagonal ground plan, which he had tried out in the Rustem Pasha Mosque in Istanbul. This enabled him to organize the interior according to a symmetry radiating from a central point. The Bazaar building, built under the forecourt, was a later gift from Murad III. The barrel-like shopping center contained 124

114

Mihrimah Mosque in Istanbul
Plan and cross section 1:500, perspective 1:1500

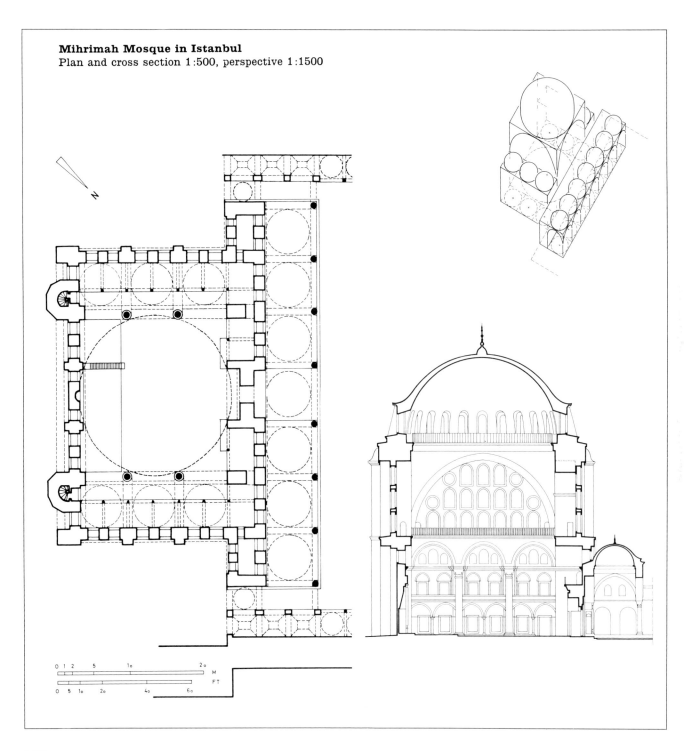

Köprülü-Yalisi in Anadoluhisari

Cross section, façade of the reception hall and plan 1:200

3. Religious and Domestic Architecture

The Exterior of Mosques

Seen from the outside, the oldest mosques in Bursa, Edirne and Istanbul were cube-shaped buildings. Gradually this cube shape was transformed into a crystal structure. Analysis of later mosques has shown that the handling of stone did not change, nor did principles of structure. The Beyazid and the Selim mosques in Istanbul are the earliest buildings in which the interior shaping begins to crystallize out of the heavy mass of the whole.

The exterior of the Şehzade Mosque gives the appearance of a single, massive block. The walls rise over and behind one another like the steps of a pyramid. The exterior gives little hint of the light, airy interior. Sinan first succeeded in fining down his walls to a thin shell in the Mihrimah Mosque. Four spires linked by four great arches carry the dome while holding the outer walls together. The exterior of St. Sophia seems mountainous compared with the exterior of Sinan's mosques. In order to decorate the interior with a layer of mosaic, everything functional which might disrupt the effect was banished to the outer walls.

In all periods of Turkish architecture the exterior of a mosque is in harmony with the interior, whether it is the complete cube of the Beyazid Mosque in Edirne, the Bursa period, or the crystalline structure of later styles. In Istanbul, the basic form of the mosque changes from the cube to the half-dome. What remains of the cube is to be found in the minarets – their slim sharp-cornered lines rising from the corners of the mosque indicate the edges of the original form.

Large gates like niches with stalactite arches continued throughout the centuries as the predominant style of the main entrance. The incursion of Gothic or Roman arches is restricted to

135

arcades ; the design of major entrances and gates remains unchanged. Indeed one would be hard put to find within the known architectural structures another form which could so absolutely nullify the impression of the weight of stone. A symbol of the frozen tension between support and downward stress, the stalactite remains the basic form for successfully carrying thrust.

Such styles and methods of Greco-Roman or Christian architecture that were adopted by the Turks were used with a certain abandon. To decorate the façade of the Süleyman Mosque's forecourt, Sinan employed the gable motif – a triangular gable supported by two half-columns. This basically tectonic design has, however, suffered a sea-change ; Sinan places the columns on stalactite bases, thereby dispelling any impression of uprightness or straightness. The gable, instead of being placed on half-columns, rests on a bracket of small icicle-like particles, like a chain of frozen raindrops. The corner pillars also seem to be at variance with their true function. Standing between similarly constructed bases and capitals, they only emphasize the fact that the stalactite niche needs no support. The design of the pillars is the same, top and bottom, dissipating any sense of dynamic vertical movement. Yet that this type of pillar was not merely intended to be an ornament, but an essential part of the structure, is proved by its repeated use in the same façade.

The structure of this façade shows the Ottoman's true regard, contrary to Western European architectural tradition, for the significance of the vertical axis.

In Turkish architecture, the cornice also serves to give a building its horizontal finality, and even follows the vertical line of the mosque's façades, linking the silhouette of the various component cube forms. This use of the cornice remains unaltered from the Beyazid Mosque in Bursa to Sinan's Selim Mosque.

Turkish Religious Architecture and Christian Traditions

The first Christian churches were built on the soil of the classical Empire. Hence, the theories of space and form which were turned to use in building churches tended to be of Roman origin. But the very different religious demands of these new churches brought about a transformation of their building styles, and out of this change grew the conflict between medieval Christian and classical building traditions which lasted until the Renaissance.

The important innovations of Greek architects had been in the investigation of the nature of stone. The Greeks had been the first to discover the laws of statics ; they had been the first to differentiate building elements according to function. The Romans continued to develop the Greek tradition with their large domed structures.

Heir to the same tradition, Christian architecture had always known the relation of the earth's gravity to tectonic problems. The Christian architect's aim, however, was not the aftermath of matter, but its conquest. Thus the relations of Christian architecture to that of classical times were always opposed.

The attempted subjection of matter took different forms in each phase of the Middle Ages. Early Christian and Byzantine architecture transforms the interior shell into smooth planes, which prevents one from perceiving any third dimension, thus lessening the impact of vault and walls.

Roman architecture, on the other hand, tends to underline the natural properties of stone – because of their structure, the walls achieve an extraordinarily compact tension, and the stone takes on a supernatural density. In Gothic architecture, statics are overcome in such a way that stone seems subject to vertical forces alone. In Turkish architecture, however, the opposition between weight and its support created no problem. Turkish buildings appear to be transcendent structures because they were designed according to a principle that was not tectonic. Whereas Gothic architecture set all forces at its disposal in motion, Turkish architecture achieved the same final harmony by freezing its forces into immobility.

This probably explains why Turkish architecture underwent no real change in style. In previous chapters we have studied works representative of a span of two hundred years. Any change observed was of a formal rather than a structural nature. The difference between the Bursa mosques and Sinan's buildings does not approach the gap separating Byzantine and Norman, Norman and Gothic. Despite large-scale formal modification of the interior, the structure of the mosque changed very little. Because Turkish religious architecture attempted to established contact with the next world by means of a state of absolute serenity, it saw no necessity to overcome forces of gravity in varying ways. Similarly, because the next world did not involve a sum of antitheses, they were not obliged to seek different ways to achieve transcendence.

Interior Decoration

The Turks and Byzantines used certain similar techniques to rid their interiors of a sense of weight. Where the Byzantines used mosaics to decorate the walls, the Turks used tiles. Both methods disguised the mass of the wall by emphasizing the smoothness of its surface. I have described the way in which this effect was achieved in an earlier book:

'The mosaic surface is made up of hundreds of opaque or semi-transparent pieces of glass or stone, which do not have even surfaces. This unevenness breaks up the light in irregular patterns, so that some of it is partly absorbed by the semi-transparent pieces and partly reflected from varying angles. The varying strength of the reflections from these tiny particles sets up an endless vibration, while the partially absorbed light makes the surface glow from within. This vibration and glow seems to separate the surface from the wall behind, allowing it to float mysteriously before our eyes. The completely even, glazed surfaces of the Turkish tiles, on the contrary, reflect the light completely, throwing it back at an equal angle. Their surface thus appears hard and impenetrable. They shine strongly without any inner glow. In contrast to the mosaic surface, they outline the body which they cover in a sharply defined way. Instead of transforming the walls into smooth surfaces, they make them into hard, glazed panes. Also, in contrast to the mosaic, they give the room solidity and coolness. Similarly, the Turks did not adopt the Byzantine custom of giving their sculptured areas pointed surfaces — like the mosaic, this was an art of disguise which used contrasts of light and dark to set up strange sensations of vibration over the walls.'

Because Byzantine artists had sought the effect of an inner glow, they preferred dark, twilight interiors. To avoid the brightness of direct sunlight in their churches, they used thin plates of yellow, glowing, semi-transparent alabaster for their windows.

Use of Light

Earlier we mentioned the Byzantine preference for ceremonies held by night. In contemporary descriptions of the interior of St. Sophia, the same preference for dawn and evening light emerges. Paulus Silentiarius's description of the inaugural ceremony emphasizes the skilful modulating of the light in different parts of the church. As the eye rises, so the light becomes brighter and brighter, attaining its full intensity at the circle of windows in the dome. Then it dims again towards the zenith of the dome which remains in darkness. We know that in those days there was a cross visible against the golden inner surface of the dome. This was replaced in late Byzantine times by a picture of Christ. The position occupied by the cross or icon was never therefore brightly illuminated, but remained in shadow. The icon glowed down out of the darkness; gloom was a necessary contrast to brightness in Byzantine interiors, in order to achieve and heighten the striking effect. According to Prokop and Silentiarius, gold, silver and precious stones were used in the furnishings of the church to give an intimation of the presence of the light of God.

These precious materials were used liberally in the Church of St. Sophia. It had been the ambition of its creator to make it a facsimile of the Heavenly Jerusalem, which in the Apocalypse appears as a city 'of pure gold and similar to pure glass.'

All this was at variance with Islamic belief. They regarded the material from which they built their mosques as being of only transient importance. Their interest in St. Sophia was therefore confined to the geometrical form. In contrast, a mosque interior is uniformly well lit. The brightness pouring in from all sides helps to emphasize the still serenity of the interior. The only increase in brightness occurs in height — that is, the floor of the mosque is the best illuminated area in the whole area. Windows reaching down to the ground light up the carpeted floor from all sides. Neither chairs nor benches disrupt the unity of this surface on which the people sit or crouch in prayer. The climax of the Mohammedan ritual prayer is to touch the floor with the forehead. To such a concept of piety, the downward shimmering 'heaven' of St. Sophia or the vertical tensions of a Gothic interior would be inappropriate.

Changes in the form of the Mosque

The influence of St. Sophia did result in changing the shape of the mosque interior from a cube to a half-dome. The cube has the property of giving no specific impulse of direction. This form changed when merged with the spherical form. In a mosque, the floor was not viewed as a solid basis of support for the structure, but rather, covered in carpets, as a free-moving area, a mirror — by touching it with the forehead, the worshipper no longer recognizes any difference between top and bottom. He sees the floor as a mirror, which gives him the feeling of being enclosed in a perfect sphere.

The Rôle of Minarets

The immutability of form, in a sense its eternity, which distinguishes Turkish religious architecture, is most clearly revealed in the style of the minarets. Their prismatic, sharply edged form is in no sense dynamic, though their pointed, slim shape may be reminiscent of the Gothic. The slender proportions of the Gothic style were the result of structural dynamics of the stone, whereas the minarets are free of any inner movement which might seek the vertical. Rather than being the result of an inner 'necessity,' like the soaring Gothic towers, one feels that the minarets were first built like an obelisk, and then hauled upright into position.

Turkish Domestic Architecture

Turkish religious and domestic architectural styles are very different and seem to have developed independently from one another. This is especially noticeable to the Westerner who is used to the history of art developing as a whole.

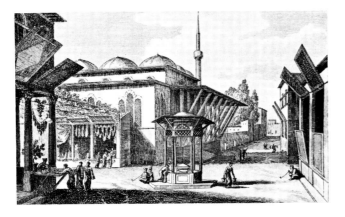

▲ Mosque and Marketplace, Gallipoli
(after a drawing by G. Fossati)

A central building, monumental dome, arches and a decorative portal are characteristic of Turkish sacred architecture. Viewed externally, their domestic architecture is, on the contrary, very plain. Houses are generally two storeys high and the rooms are asymmetrically planned. In houses with symmetrical plans, the symmetry is hardly visible on the façades. The external characteristics of the Turkish dwellings are the broad, projecting tent shaped roofs, covered with red tiles. There is no evidence of vault, arch or portal. Styles are based on straight, especially horizontal lines. Unlike religious architecture, stone was seldom employed in domestic buildings, with the exception of the southern regions. Even where stone was plentiful, it was rarely used to build houses.

Plans of the Turkish Dwelling

Two factors were considered in the design of the Turkish house :

1) The geographical nature of the region.

2) The Islamic custom of women only being allowed to meet the men of the family when veiled. This accounted for the strict division between men's and women's quarters. Moreover, the very varied geographical nature of Asia Minor accounts for numerous differences in the types of houses.

The custom of providing separate entrances, staircases and quarters for men and women applied to all parts of the country, and without social distinction. Even houses consisting of only two rooms were divided into a 'harem' (women's quarters) and a 'selamlik' (men's quarters). The master and the mistress dined and entertained guests separately in their own apartments. Also universally typical was the absolute uniformity of the rooms. Europeans have always planned each room according to its function and then furnished them accordingly. Turkish homes had no such arrangement ; furniture such as beds, tables or chairs were not confined to one room. Nor was there any difference between the furnishing of men's and women's quarters. Every room was interchangeable ; from living-to-dining-to-bedroom. Rooms were mostly divided into two parts : the entrance and the actual living part, built on a slightly higher level than the former. In wealthier homes, the entrance was enclosed by wooden pillars and a balustrade. The floor here was covered with mats on which a person entering had to leave his shoes. The entrance was also for servants. The custom of exchanging shoes for slippers when entering the mosque was also observed in private homes.

At least one wall of the living-quarter had a

continuous row of windows. The other walls contained built-in cupboards, open shelves and small niches for various items – tables were not customary. Deep built-in cupboards along the entrance walls were used for bedding, cotton mattresses, quilts and pillows were rolled up in the morning and placed in these cupboards. The room was converted into a dining room by placing a large brass or copper tray on a low stool, which was then used as a table. One ate from this table, seated on floor cushions. The only other piece of furniture was the 'sedir,' a long, low, wide divan, set in the window wall. Carpets and soft cushions added to the general comfort, and the room was heated when necessary by a charcoal stove in the center.

There were no connecting doors between rooms ; each room was a complete unit. The single entrance doors were small and narrow, and were usually so designed that the room was not wholly visible from the outside when the door was opened.

The Arrangement of the Rooms

The houses in Anatolia and the Balkan provinces generally had asymmetric plans. The symmetrical plan, with a large central hall running through the whole house, was only typical of wealthier homes in Istanbul.

The simplest plan consists of a hall with a few rooms to one side. Often the rooms were grouped around the hall in a 'L' or 'U' shape – this according to the owner's wealth or needs. The ground floor has few living-rooms and contains the cellar, store-rooms, kitchen and servant quarters.

The entrance to the house was usually reached through a garden or courtyard and from there an open wooden staircase – in larger houses two staircases – led to the hall on the

first floor. In many regions the hall was open on one side. In cooler regions, the stairs led to a pergola from which one entered a glazed hall.

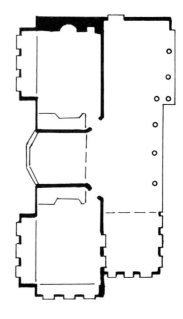

▲ House in Edirne: Plan (after S. H. Eldem)

The hall, or sofa, was one of the most important rooms in the house. During the summer, particularly, it was the place most frequented by

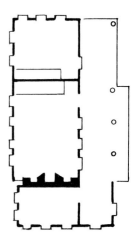

House in Antalya: Plan
(after S. H. Eldem)

the family. An airy half-open room leading to shaded inner gardens or, as in Istanbul summer houses, a long central room entirely walled with windows, the hall was the coolest room in the house. For the women especially, who spent most of their time indoors, the hall was the only place where they could make contact with nature. In Anatolian houses there was often a glazed pavilion at the end of the hall, which formed a corner room with a view over the street. These rooms were especially popular during summer.

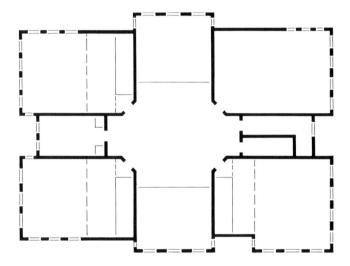

▲ House in Babek, on the Bosporus:
Plan (after S. H. Eldem)

Clearly the corner room was always the best room in the house. On the Anatolian plateau, where there are extremes of summer and winter temperatures, it was customary to distinguish between summer and winter rooms. Winter rooms usually faced south, had smaller windows and lower ceilings. In hilly cities like Bursa or Ankara, winter rooms were situated on the mezzanine floor. This seasonal change did not interfere with the family's way of life, since the servant quarters and the kitchen, as well as, often, the toilets, were on the ground floor, accessible from the garden and therefore not

directly connected to the actual living rooms.

Although the Turkish room possessed hardly any furniture, it was by no means bare or dull.

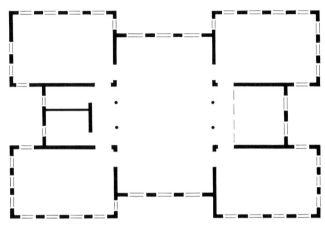

▲ Garden Pavillion in Kula: Plan (after S. H. Eldem)

Without furniture, carpets become a very important part of the room. The colorful carpet usually formed a warm contrast with the wooden, finely decorated ceiling. Between these two richly colorful horizontal areas, the room extended uninterrupted. The wide divans stretching along the windows increased the effect of spaciousness. In this way the smallest room seems generously proportioned.

The grouping of the windows as well as their shape emphasizes the horizontal effect. With few exceptions, windows are divided into two parts: the lower half is a sash window, the upper, which does not open, has stained-glass panes and plaster decoration. The lower parts are latticed, thus making it impossible for the women to be seen from outside. The combination of lattice and glass affect the lighting of the room, in spite of the numerous windows: the lower part of the room seems shadowed, but it grows increasingly bright towards the ceiling.

Room of a house in
Antalya: Plan
(after S. H. Eldem)

Room of a house in
Mudanya: Plan
(after S. H. Eldem)

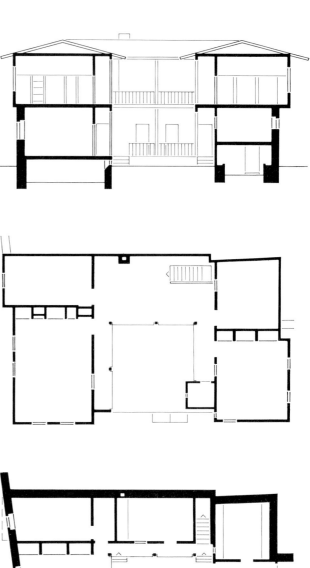

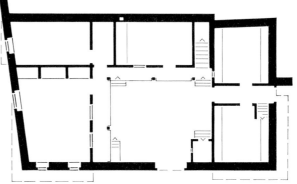

The multi-colored light coming through the stained-glass brings out the decorations on the wood ceiling. The way in which light is filtered into the room increases its atmosphere of intimacy.

Another very typical feature of the Turkish house is its alcoves. A whole street becomes distinctive because of these rows of alcoves. They project over the almost windowless street-level walls, supported on steep wooden buttresses. And while the lattices prevented the passerby from looking in, they did not prevent the inhabitants from looking out. Women could follow daily life on the street from the alcoves by looking through small openings fitted into the intricate pattern of the lattice-work.

The plans of single-storeyed detached garden pavilions also show alcove-like projections with continuous rows of windows. Buildings such as these, needing neither angular compensation nor artificial increase in their lighting, could only have been built with the intention of obtaining as wide a view as possible. The pavilions had no need of lattices. Despite the hot summers, large, open windows were built, since the tent like roof offered the necessary broad area of shade.

From these basic requirements – bright rooms and good views – Turkish architecture created two types of building: the Yali and the Köschk They are the most significant achievements in domestic architecture. The Yali is a seaside residence, located in much the same way as were later Venetian palaces. The Köschk is a single-storeyed, detached pavilion found in the gardens of the wealthy residences or in beautiful parks. In these buildings the architect could give his imagination free rein, something that was not always possible in a town.

The Yali

This type originated in Istanbul on the shores of the Bosporus. A symmetrical plan, with a large central living room extending the length of the whole building, was typical of these summer residences. Rooms, as usual, were only 'provisionally' furnished: furnishing of rooms in the European style begins only after the middle of the nineteenth century.

Styles and construction of alcoves in the yali were new and daring, proving that the alcove was not merely a functional requirement. One of the Istanbul Turk's most cherished habits was to sit in this alcove, projecting over the water, and enjoy the panoramic beauty of the surroundings.

The Köprülü-Yalisi in Anadoluhisari

Most of the old Yalis on the Bosporus have now-

▼ Street in a suburb of Istanbul, c. 1850
(after a drawing by G. Fossati)

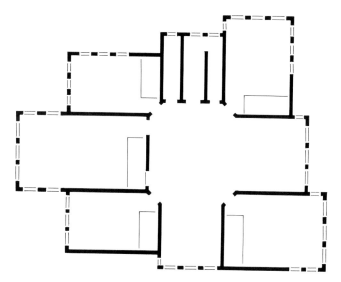

▲ Yali in Cengelköy, on the Bosporus:
Plan (after S. H. Eldem)

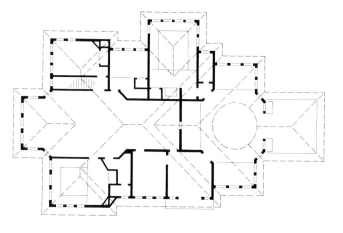

▲ Aynali-Kavak-Kasiri, on the Golden Horn:
Plan (after S. H. Eldem)

adays been demolished or have been so changed
by restoration that they bear little relation to
their original appearance. One of the few exceptions is the reception room of the Köprülü-Yali,
a building that dates from the end of the seventeenth century. (The adjoining rooms have not
been preserved.)

This room is shaped like a Latin cross with
three cross-axes, which partly extend over the

▲ The Köprülü-Yalisi in Anadoluhisari, on the Bosporus:
Perspective of the reception hall

water, and which form the alcoves with low
sedirs around the walls. The windows, unlike the
usual designs, are bipartite, and upper windows
are replaced by a decorated wall of wood. The
wall was a kind of cover for the sash-windows
which, when open, seemed to disappear completely, thus giving one the impression of
being in a room that floated over the water.
Horizontally divided shutters that folded up-
wards and downwards regulated light and air,
and were typical of the waterside façades of the
Yalis.

The three alcoves are lined with carpets. The
square area in the center is floored in marble,
and was used as an ante-room. A fountain with a
square base is the only decoration. The ceiling
is vaulted, whereas the alcoves have the usual
level, richly decorated wooden ceilings. The
marble floor and the fountain were also found in
more modest summer residences.

The 'Köschk' or 'Kasir'

The garden pavilion and summerhouse, which the Turks call Köschk or Kasir, were actually part of the palace and were not, as in Europe, small additions of merely architectural significance. They were detached buildings containing

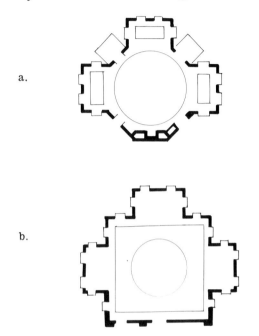

a.

b.

▲ a. Revan-Köschkü in the garden of the Top Kapi Seray
b. Sepetçiler-Köschkü in the garden of the Top Kapi Seray: Plans (after S. H. Eldem)

one to three rooms. Many of the Turkish Sultans' residences consisted of several of these single-storey buildings set in shaded gardens. The earliest palace was at Edirne, but few traces of it exist today, and it has been replaced by the Selim Mosque. Murad II began building a new palace on the island of Tundscha at Edirne, but this was only completed in the reign of Mohamed II. After the conquest of Constantinople, Mohamed spent some time at the Edirne palace, and later Süleyman and his son, Selim, added to it. Successive Sultans restored and extended it, and the palace was used until the end of the eighteenth century.

The Turks destroyed the palace themselves – retreating before a Russian advance in 1878 which was to occupy Edirne. What little remains, however, gives us an idea of the general lay-out, and this is supplemented by sketches that two French artists, Desernod and Sayger, made before the palace was destroyed. Desernod and Sayger visited Edirne at the beginning of the nineteenth century. They published their sketches in 1829 but these were accompanied, unfortunately, by only a few footnotes.

A fairly exact description was found among the letters of General Helmuth von Moltke, who had been in Edirne in 1837. He wrote: 'The old Seray still exists; I visited it today with great interest. The locality, a beautiful meadow on the Tundscha, overshadowed by great plane trees and elms, does not lend itself to building a house, since all the surroundings are flooded in winter. High walls enclose a fairly extensive area, over which are scattered various buildings: individual residences, baths, kitchens and pavilions, each forming a different court of the palace. A few are still well-preserved and have very beautiful designed and richly gilded ceilings, marble baths and wood carving. At the center of the complex is a massive stone building with a strange tower – its walls are still largely covered with exquisite porcelain tiles. The building has been so solidly constructed that it might well stand for some thousands of years: but it is very large, and resembles the saray in Constantinople, in that one looks in vain among so many pavilions for the actual main building.' The building with 'the strange tower' was the residence of Mohamed II, and was called Gihannuma-Kasari (world-view pavilion) because of the observation room at the top.

The Gihannuma-Kasari, with its block-line appearance and twenty-one rooms, is unusual in Turkish palace architecture. The function of the polygonal tower was merely to provide the Sultan with a higher observation room. According to old descriptions it was some 70 feet high and had 142 steps leading to the summit. The floor in this top room was tiled in marble and, despite technical difficulties, the room contained a

▲ The Gihannuma-Kasiri in Edirne:
General View

fountain. The furnishing consisted of low benches along the walls. Here Mohamed II retired, either alone or with his poets and intellectuals.

One of the most beautiful buildings on this site was the so called Kum-Kasari. This single-storeyed building east of the Gihannuma pavilion, served as a residence and school for princes. Built at the time of the conquest of Constantinople, it was renovated and transformed in the seventeenth century according to current fash-

ion. Sketches by Desernod and Sayger show it after the renovation. Kum-Kasari was a wood building containing two large and three smaller rooms. The latter form the right wing of the pavilion, which was used in winter. Here the walls were thicker, the windows smaller and

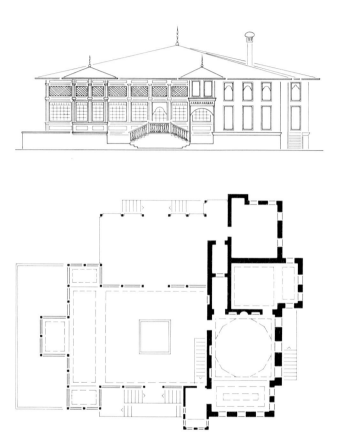

▲ Kum-Kasiri in Edirne: Façade and plan
(after Desernod and Sayger)

fewer in number. Each room contained a fireplace. The two larger rooms were intended for summer use and each was accessible from the garden. The floors were covered with marble tiles. One of the larger rooms had a pool with a

▲ Terrace of a café on the Bosporus, c. 1850
(after a drawing by G. Fossati)

fountain, and alcove-like projections in three directions. The windows were so constructed that they could be removed during hot weather, thus transforming the rooms into open halls, consisting only of slender wooden posts and a canvas roof.

Early documents state that the saray site at Edirne contained a total of 119 rooms. Besides many pavilions, summer houses, kitchens and storerooms, twenty-two baths and thirteen mesdschid (small single-roomed mosques) are also listed. There were additional pavilions reserved for the sick, together with a maternity hospital. Old drawings show that the Sultan's throne-room, conference and reception rooms were similar in design to the Kum-Kasari.

The Top Kapi Saray in Istanbul

Istanbul's old palace stood on the site which is now occupied by the university, between the Beyazid and the Süleyman mosques. It was not until twenty years after the conquest of Constantinople that the building of a large palace was begun.

The spit of land between the Golden Horn and the Sea of Marmara was chosen as the site for the new palace. As at Edirne, this saray was to be not only a residence, but also a center of government and culture. The Top Kapi evolved from the various additions made to the palace by Sultans over the centuries. Consequently we should not consider it as a single unit, but trace its gradual development. Yet despite the passage of time, we shall see that the conception of living hardly changed.

The site is divided into three courtyards. The final one leads onto a terrace-like garden that offers a splendid view of town and harbor. Strict axial order is lacking in the grouping of the single buildings around the courts, yet the arrangement of the different buildings according to their function is by no means accidental. The selection of sites for the various groups of buildings seems to have developed from the practical to the intellectual, or from the public and representative to the intimate.

The first gate, Babi-Hûmayan (Imperial Gate) opens onto the first court, a large flat area intended for ceremonial parades and exercises. To the left of this area were workshops, storerooms and stables and further on, the law court and other administrative buildings. On the right of the gate was the Ministry of Finance. The central court was reached from the second gate through a narrow, low building. In addition to guard rooms, this gate house also contained prison cells, intended for deposed statesmen. The execution block and the 'executioner's well' stood immediately in front of the gate. Statesmen passed this place on their way to the council chambers: significantly, the block was called 'the stone of warning.'

The principal building in the second court contained the council chambers. A path led from the second gate directly to the building, and the court was distinguished from the others with their unbroken rows of arcades by its higher dome and vestibule. Hidden behind these arcades, however, were buildings of various sizes and purposes. To the right were kitchens and bakeries, and to the left, stables and accommodation for the Sultan's household. The Sultan's private apartments and the harem were immediately behind the council chambers, and the Sultan could enter the council chamber directly from his apartments.

The entrances to the harem are in the third court. The gate to this last court was called 'the gate of happiness.' The only 'official' room in the court was the Arz-Odasi, the audience chamber. The Sultan received foreign ambassadors here: it was a single-storeyed building containing only one large room. The harem extends along the left side of the court, and over the centuries this side has become one large complex formed from various large rooms, halls and courtyards.

A few schoolrooms and the imperial kitchen completed the court on the left side. Two further buildings – a mosque and a library – are placed separately within the courtyard, immediately behind the audience chamber. This court, too, has an unbroken row of arcades, so constructed as to give the courtyard a uniform façade. A small path opposite the audience chamber leads to the Sultan's private gardens, which overlook the Golden Horn, the harbor, the Bosporus, the Asiatic coast and the Sea of Marmara.

Pavilions and Summerhouses

The terraced garden contained various pavilions and summer-houses, most of which were small buildings with alcoves and balconies, simply but expensively decorated. The terrace between the Baghdad Köschkü and the Sunnet Köschkü (Circumcision Chamber) has the best view. The Baghdad Köschkü is an octagonal building with four large alcoves surmounted by a wide-eaved roof supported by arcades. It is situated on the north-east corner of the farthest terrace, and its balconies and alcoves project seawards beyond the steep slope. Murad II erected this in 1633 to mark the occasion of the conquest of Baghdad, and this accounts for the interior decor reminiscent of Arabic homes. A large observation terrace connects the Baghdad Köschkü with the Sunnet Köschkü. These two buildings, the observation terrace and the neighboring Revan-Köschkü are the most interesting group on the whole site.

A typical observation building is the Kara-Mustafa Pasha Köschkü, on the right of the Baghdad group. This consists of a rectangular block, level when viewed from the garden side, which projects partly over the terrace and is supported by wooden pillars. The walls are made almost wholly of glass. Apart from the halls and pillars of the Aynali Kavak Kasiri on the Golden Horn, this interior is one of the most typical examples of eighteenth-century Köschk architecture.

This short survey of the two largest palaces has clearly shown that Ottoman palace architecture does not differ considerably from that of middle-class houses, either in the selection of building material or in the dimensions of the rooms. With their richly decorated ceilings and walls, their valuable carpets and hangings, the interiors are not commonplace – yet neither are they stiff or ceremonious. The palaces are almost always single-storeyed and their dimensions and proportions are suitably modest. Yet this certainly does not suggest a prevailing democratic view and, even less, a lack of consciousness of power: the Sultan's large mosques and Külliyes speak for themselves – they underline the self-assurance of the Ottoman period. That even the Sultan should observe the temporary nature of life is a fundamental part of religious belief –

and we have seen how this is related to Turkish town-planning. Since life on earth is merely transitory, a house should not assume monumental significance. Nothing is lasting or indestructible. In this context, it is interesting to note that it was customary to leave a small part of the house unfurnished.

We have noticed how the need for the greatest possible view influenced the design of the living-rooms. We should undoubtedly be wrong in attributing this wholly to the needs of the women who were confined to the harem, since neither the Gihannuma tower of Mohamed II, nor the reception room of the Köprülü-Yalisi were intended for women. The strange style of the Gihannuma tower and the daring alcoves of the Köprülü-Yalisi also resulted from this desire for the best possible view. These buildings were consequently named 'world view' or 'Beauty of the World.'

Western Influence during the Nineteenth Century

With the exception of the segregation of women's and men's quarters, life as described in the previous chapter may still be found today in some Anatolian towns. In large cities, Istanbul or Izmir, Western influences were already noticeable during the nineteenth century. The West, mainly France, influenced the wave of reform in 1839, known as the Fanzimat (New Order). The slow trend to the West began at this time and not, as is commonly believed, after World War I and the subsequent revolution in 1922. 1922 did see the complete break with Islamic tradition but the roots of this revolution lie in the Fanzimat. The Fanzimat was a far-seeing precaution against the increasingly urgent demands of the Western powers. Their demands were related to the Christian minority of the country which, according to the West, was oppressed by the Islamic legal system. In order to avoid further interference from the West, the Turks tried to resolve the differences between the various sects, who because of different beliefs, had up till the present remained disunited.

This was Turkey's first step towards relaxing Islamic laws for civil rights and education. From this time onwards, absolute Islamic power receded: the foundation of a University on Western lines was the first indication of the new school of thought. The interest in western languages and life became increasingly popular and during these years a large number of western literary masterpieces were translated.

In architecture, too, the new way of life was accompanied by new social establishments: schools, hospitals, government offices and law courts – all based on the European pattern. Although the private home was not affected, its interior was adapted to European tastes, particularly in fashionable circles. Furnishing in western style had already begun around the middle of the nineteenth century. (Rococo and Empire furniture did not appear until a few decades later.)

Commissions for large palaces in Baroque and Rococo styles were much sought after by nineteenth-century architects. Baroque influence was noticeable in Turkish architecture by the middle of the eighteenth century (the Nuru-Osman Mosque and the Lalel Mosque in Istanbul). Western architectural influence mainly affected style and ornamentation; the internal organization of individual buildings and, certainly, the way of life were never affected.

Plates

Istanbul

Top Kapi Seray

155 **The Sunnet-Köschkü.** View of the exterior and the terrace.

156 Entrance hall. The glazed doors are of a later period. The arches were originally not filled in with glass.

157 View into the interior. The lack of furniture seems to enlarge the sense of space.

158 A sitting-corner. The colorful ceiling, tiled walls and the flower motifs on the bench covers give the room a pleasant atmosphere.

159 **The Kara Mustafa Pasha Köschkü.** View from the garden.

160 Interior, looking towards the sea. Baroque and Rococo influence is visible in the decoration.

161 Detail of the frontal façade. On the sea, the building extends outwards over the terraces, and is supported by wooden pillars.

162 Harem. Bedroom of Murad III (1574-1595).

163 **Köprülü-Yalisi.** Exterior view of the reception hall. This is the oldest example of the remaining Yalis on the Bosporus.

164 Interior of the reception hall, looking south.

165 Detail of the southern projection.

Konya

166 **Dwelling house:** entrance and hall leading directly to the rooms. Single-storey building, with earth covered roof.

167 Interior of a room.

Bursa

168 **Yeni-Kaplica.** Exterior view. Founded by the Grand Vizier Rustem Pasha. The external walls of the bathing rooms were undecorated. The marble wall which encloses the building at the rear is a later addition.

169 Interior of the Tepidarium.

170 Dome of the hot-room. The windowless bathing rooms were lit by glass 'eyes' let into the dome.

Site plan of Top Kapi Seray 1:2000

1   Main gate
2   Kitchen
3   Kubbe Alti (Council Chamber)
4   Harem wing
5   Side gate
6   Arz-Odasi (Audience Chamber)
7   Library
8   Kara Mustafa Pasha Köschkü
9   Sunnet-köschkü (Circumcision Chamber)
10 Revan-köschkü
11 Bagdad-köschkü

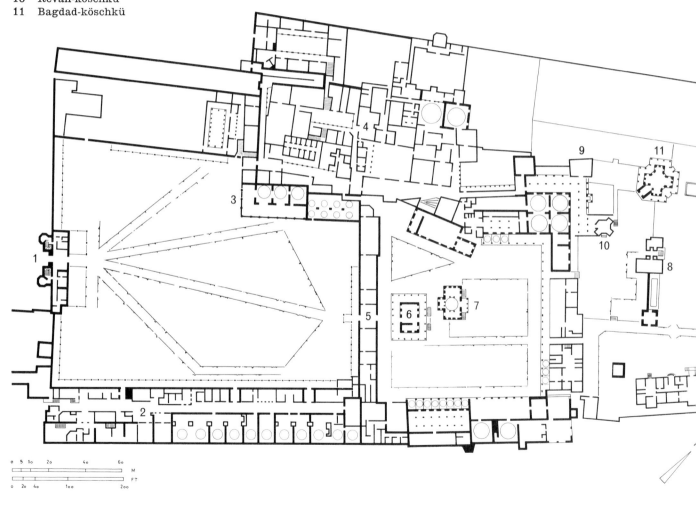

152

Kara Mustafa-köschkü in the garden of the Top Kapi Seray

(No. 8 in plan)

Plan, cross section and elevation 1:250

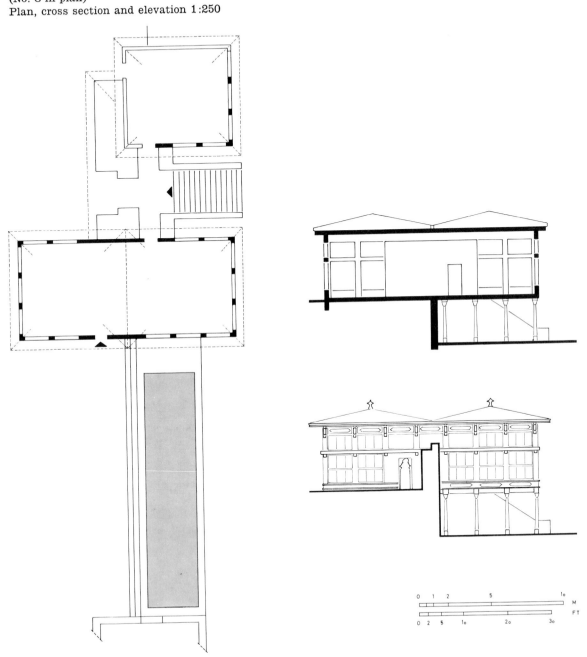

Notes

Istanbul

Top Kapi Seray was begun by Mohamed I some twenty years after the conquest of Constantinople. Extended in the eighteenth century. The site stretches from St. Sophia to the Seray promontory between the Sea of Marmara and the Golden Horn. The Sunnet Köschkü and the Kara Mustafa Pasha pavilion are on the farthest terrace, with a superb view of the city.

The Sunnet Köschkü is a seventeenth-century building. It was the royal circumcision hall.

The Kara Mustafa Köschkü is a single-roomed building, renovated in 1752. The windows are as deep as doors, the walls almost entirely of glass. Certain western influences are already visible here.

The Köprülü-Yalisi is in Anadolihisari on the Asian bank of the Bosporus, and was built at the end of the seventeenth century. Only the reception hall remains. The builder was Huseyin Pasha, one of the Köprülü family of viziers. He was successively Governor of Istanbul, Chief Admiral and Grand Vizier. The reception hall, half of which was built over the water, has an unique view of both sides of the Bosporus. Note the lack of upper windows.

Konya

Dwelling House. The building style reflects the climate, with its sudden extreme changes in temperature. The rooms are grouped round a central garden. The building material is coarse brick. A layer of earth on the roof acts as another protective layer against heat or frost. The houses are mostly single-storeyed.

Bursa

The Yeni-Kaplica : Built during the rule of the Grand Vizier, Rustem Pasha. Cured here of his disease, Süleyman I vowed to build a medicinal bath, and this was incorporated into Rustem Pasha's foundation.

The plan is usual, with one exception – the hot-room has a large pool in the center. Because this was a thermal and therefore medicinal bath, one was permitted to bathe in it, contrary to usual religious requirements.

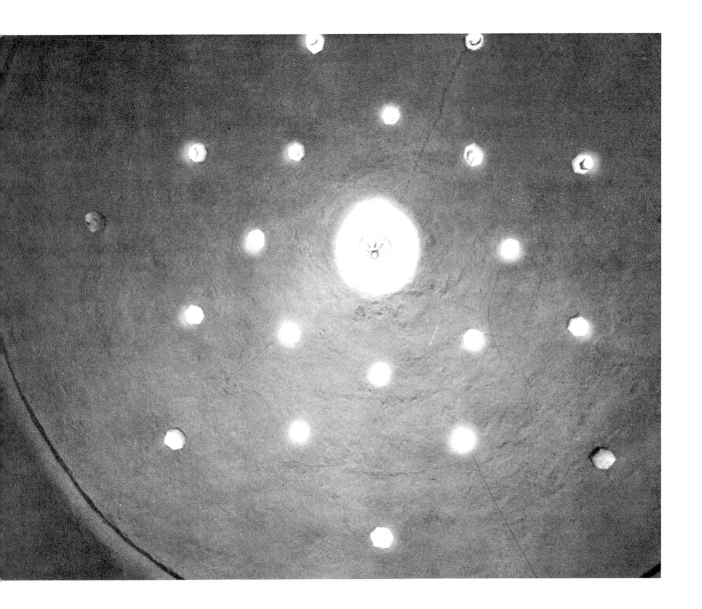

House in Konya
Cross section and plan 1:200

Detail of wall and window construction
Cross section 1:100

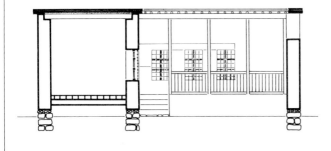

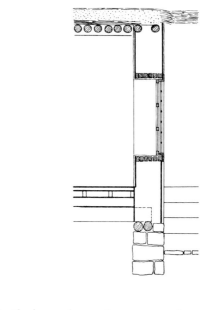

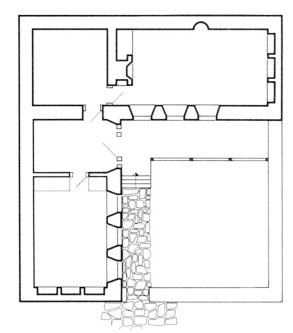

Yeni-Kaplica in Bursa
Section 1:500, plan and perspective 1:1000

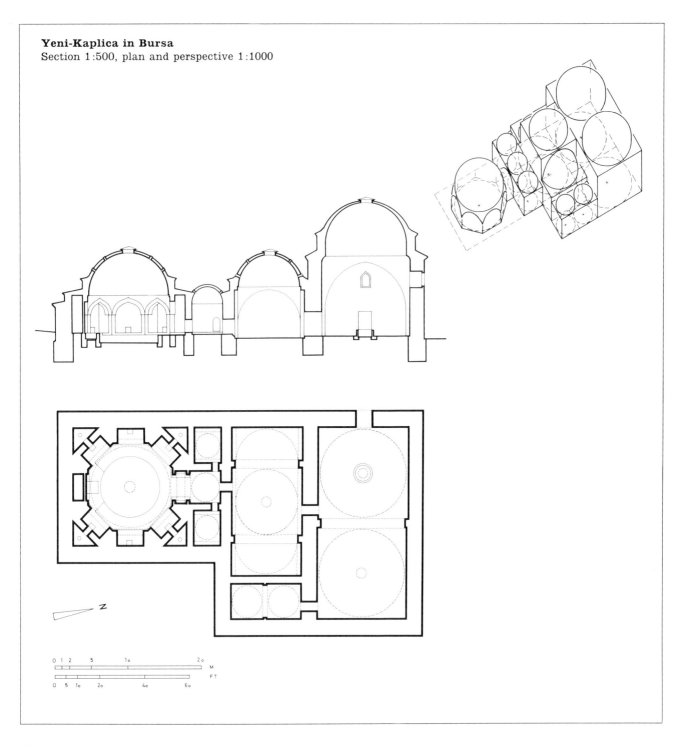

4. Baths and Caravanserai

Baths

The donation of public baths (hamam) was an ancient Ottoman tradition. Architecturally, the hamam did not always form part of the actual Külliye, and was usually found close by : another gift from the same donor.

The oldest hamam in Bursa, erected on the site of a former Byzantine thermal building, was donated by Murad I and was most probably built by the architect of Murad I's Külliye. The basic form of the Turkish hamam is already evident here : an entrance hall, tepidarium and a hot-room. This form continued until the eighteenth century, with only small variations.

Karl Klinghardt, the first to study hamams in Istanbul and Asia Minor, noticed that Turkish bath installations have very little in common with those of their Byzantine predecessors. He draws attention to the fact that the installation of baths was usual in Asian countries, Russia, Bulgaria and Mongolia. Moreover, the Ottomans had brought the bath to Asia Minor from their Near Eastern home.

The Koran too, had something to say on bathing, and it bears little relation to Byzantine or Western concepts : it states that only running water is cleansing. Before entering the mosque, before prayer and the reading of the Koran, a man must always bathe – but only with running water. Therefore, dialectically speaking, washing in a bathtub or swimming in a pool does not make a man clean. Thus, except for the thermal baths, Turkish baths do not consist of bathtubs or pools ; and even in the thermal baths, regulations dictated that one must clean the body thoroughly before entering the pool. Once washed – a rite administered according to strict regulations – prayer might begin. Because the Mohammedan is obliged to observe the Namaz (prayers) five times a day, he had to wash him-

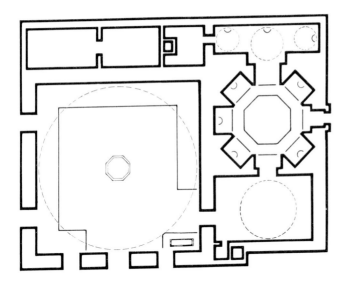

▲ Bit-Pazar Hamam in Bursa:
Plan (after K. Klinghardt)

self correspondingly often. The washing consisted of five actions : washing of the hands and forearms up to the elbow ; washing of the face ; wetting of a quarter of the head ; and, finally, washing of the feet. This is carried out in a particular order, and accompanied by prayers. The sequence, if interrupted, had to be recom

menced. Thorough washing could only be achieved in a bath, since it was also necessary to observe the rule that no part of the body should remain dry. Because the bath was thus so intimately connected with religion, the hamam achieved status in the eyes of religious, rich Mohammedans who wanted to become famous donors.

The building of large-scale public baths was not customary, but smaller public baths abounded. The regular visit to the baths was one of the contry's most typical national habits. Evliya Celebi notes that during his lifetime (around the mid-seventeenth century) about 150 public baths existed in Istanbul. The hamams increased mainly because of religious beliefs, but also, to a lesser extent, because of a desire for social recreation. Their function can therefore hardly be compared with the role played by the large thermal baths of ancient Byzantine, where Roman tradition had been continued. With their large pools and lavish decorations, the halls of the Byzantine baths were more than merely functional : they were places where society might meet for entertainment. Turkish hamams

Ingile-Hamam in Bursa:
Section ▼ and plan ▶ (after K. Klinghardt)

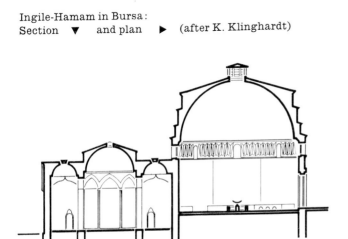

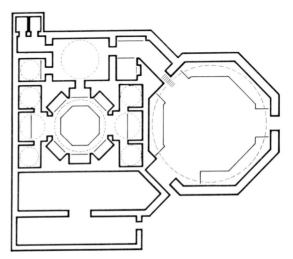

never went beyond being purely functional – not even during the most brilliant period of the Ottoman Empire – and their interiors remained modest. Two kinds of hamams developed: the Thermal Bath (Kaplica or Ilica) and the Public Bath. Architecturally, the types are similar. The order of the rooms is the same, although the thermal baths differ in that they have a pool in the center of the last room. The public baths were single or double, and followed the established sequence of rooms. The double baths were separated for women and men, and so allowed them to visit the baths at any time during the day. Single baths reserved three days a week for women only.

▲ Corner structure from the baths in Bursa
(after K. Klinghardt)

Turkish architects did not give as much attention to the exteriors of the hamams as to those of mosques. Many city hamams are not even detached buildings. Tucked away between houses, they are only recognizable by their entrance, similar to a present-day cinema. Detached hamams have no windows, their interiors being lit by means of glass 'eyes' inserted in the dome.

The Use of Various Rooms

The entrance hall was used for receiving clients, for changing, and was the largest room in the building. It equalled the size of the whole site, and could consist of one or more interconnecting rooms. Along the walls were slightly raised (5 to 8 feet) broad balconies, covered with mats and carpets, where clients could rest after their bath and acclimatize themselves to the cooler atmosphere. In larger hamams the walls were lined with two-storeyed wooden galleries. The upper storey contained private cubicles or rooms for the more distinguished clients.

The Tepidarium

The second room, the tepidarium, was moderately

▼ Detail of a dome with a glass 'eye'
(after K. Klinghardt)

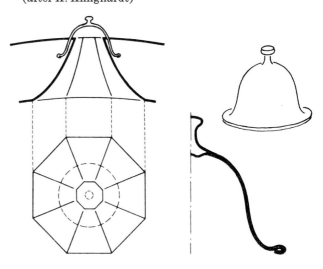

heated so that the visitor could get used to the heat. In accordance with Islamic beliefs, toilets and depilatory cubicles were to be found off this intermediate room.

The third room was the hot-room. It was a domed octagonal hall, around which were open recesses containing water basins. Along the walls were low marble benches. A stone table of the same height served as a massage table. Immediately behind the hot-room was the boiler-room.

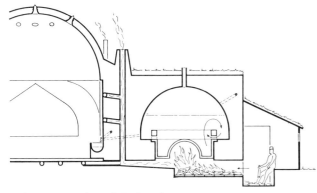

▲ Reconstruction of the heating system (after K. Klinghardt)

The Heating Arrangements

The boiler-room was at the rear of the building. The intermediate and hot-rooms were heated by hot air which circulated under the floor's stone tiles. The fireplace in the boiler-room was at a lower level than the floors of the other rooms. The fire heated water in a huge kettle and steam was distributed to the other rooms by means of channels. The temperature of the hottest room fluctuated between $30°$ c and $40°$ c but in private cubicles next to the boiler room it was much hotter.

Yeni Kaplica

Hammer-Purgstall, who visited the Yeni-Kaplica on his journey to Bursa, was very impressed by this beautiful hamam. He wrote : 'Yeni Kaplica, the new hamam, the most outstanding and beautiful of its kind, is situated between the old hamam and the town. Like the old hamam its dome is lead-covered. The facing of the walls and the plaster on the floor, which reflect the light from above, make it unique . . . The pool is huge, and water once flowed out of the jaws of a marble lion, which is no longer there. Perhaps this was an imitation of the famous lion fountain in Granada.'

'Gurur etme libass fahrile Omre hadschandur,
Bu Kâbei cismi gör bunda herkes camekândur.'
This Turkish inscription is in the dressing room of the Yeni-Kaplica, and translated, reads :
'Do not be proud of clothes, for what is life ?
A room in which all must leave their cloaks.'
It is further proof of the Islamic indifference towards earthly possessions and class distinction. The epigrams were often inscribed in the hamam and also in the caravanserai.

Interiors

The entrance hall was a large high rectangular room, consisting of two equal-sized square units. A high pointed arch, formed from two segments of a circle, connects the two rooms, each of which has a dome. The entrance to the ante-room is on the shorter side of the rectangle. In the center of the first room is a fountain, the only ornament in the whole hall. From here a low opening, vaulted with Roman arches, leads to the tepidarium.

This second room repeats the proportions of the entrance hall, although on a smaller scale. Its ceiling consists of a central dome flanked by two half-domes. Adjoining the right and shorter side of the tepidarium are two low, square, domed rooms which were most probaly used as private changing rooms (today they are merely used for storing equipment). Between the tepidarium and the hot-room is a tripartite spacing with three equal sized low domes, the middle of which forms a kind of wind-breaker for the hot-room; the two side rooms, only accessible from the intermediate room, were used as private baths.

The hot-room has a regular octagonal plan. We have dealt mainly with the mineral bath, and we find here a large round pool in the center. Seven walls of the octagon are built as niches, each of which contains a water basin. The exterior walls in this building are, as usual, rectangular in shape. Since the interior is squared, four triangular rooms remain behind the corner niches. They are accessible by low doors in the rear niche walls and were used as private baths.

The wall structure of the hamam is irregular. In the entrance hall, the completely uniform surface of the walls is broken by three high windows with pointed arches. The room is lit mainly by the large glass 'eyes' set at the top of the dome. Equally simple is the wall structure in the tepidarium. Here, as well as in the entrance hall, the transition from quadrangle to circle is formed by straight pendentives.

From an architectural point of view, the last room forms the climax of the whole building. It seems more complex because of its polygonal plan and different sized niches topped by pointed arches. The play of octagon, rectangle and circle embellishes the room, although the principle of simple straight walls was adhered to. This room is made beautiful by the floor mosaics and tiled walls.

Similar to rich carpets on a white marble floor, rectangles filled with red, yellow and black stones reflect the light from the glass 'eyes' above. Radiating from a twelve-pointed star in the center, the 'stone carpet' forms an arabesque-like pattern.

Decoration extends about six feet up the walls. Similar to the wall decoration of the Yeschil-Cami, it consists of hexagonal and triangular tiles. Each niche has a different pattern. Only the walls of the niche opposite the entrance, bearing the donor's plaque, are tiled to the ceiling.

External Aspect of the Hamam

The building consists of one, or from one to three, cube shaped rooms, placed side by side. The order – entrance and changing room, tepidarium and hot-room – is always the same. The architect was, however, free to do what he liked with the structure as a whole. There are two reasons for this: first, since the hot-room was only lit from the roof, the architect did not, as in other buildings, have to take side-lighting into consideration; secondly, the likely loss of heat resulted in other buildings being 'wrapped' around the hamam. This is why façades or the cube-like shape does not, externally, play an important rôle. Although the Yeni-Kaplica is a detached building, the entrance hall is, none-the-less, the only external important feature. The remainder consists of a heavy stolid mass of wall. Yet a comparison of different haman buildings designed by skilful architects reveals much innovation in the cube-hemisphere character of the rooms. Especially interesting in this connection are the so-called Cifte-Hamam, the double baths for men and women, which have the same sequence of rooms. The intimate and relaxing atmosphere of these rooms is not only due to their relatively small size but also – and chiefly – to their unrestricted character.

The Han (Caravanseray)

The East possessed no equivalent to today's hotels with comfortable rooms and restaurants.

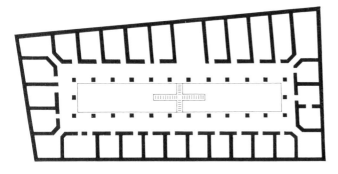

▲ Rustem Pasha Han in Istanbul: Plan

Bey-Han in Istanbul: Plan　　　　　　　▶

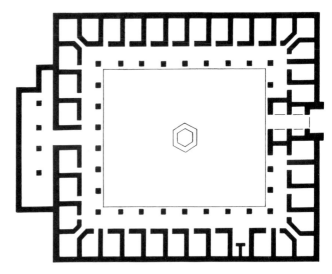

From the Middle Ages to the beginning of this century the han was the Orient's only form of inn. Hans were built to give travelers overnight lodging. They can be found in cities and at intervals of one day's journey on the roads. On caravan routes there was a more luxurious type, called caravanseray – medieval equivalents of the modern motel.

The caravanserai in Persian and Seljuk times were monumental stone buildings with enormous pillars and vaults. A small mosque raised on four arches, for communal prayer, was to be found in the center of the courtyard. Although the Seljuk Han was fairly common in Anatolia, the Ottoman Turks did not continue this architectural style. As with the medrese and hamam the Turks considered the han as merely functional and so reduced its size and shape. Ottoman architecture rarely produced innovations in the han building.

The first hans of the Ottoman period can be found in Bursa. Their simple external appearance does not indicate that they had lost their importance during Ottoman rule. On the contrary, because of the Ottoman's development,

economy as well as trade suddenly boomed. The many early Ottoman hans in Bursa are alone proof of this. The city hans in particular acquired a new commercial character during the

▼ Hasan Pasha Han in Istanbul: Plan

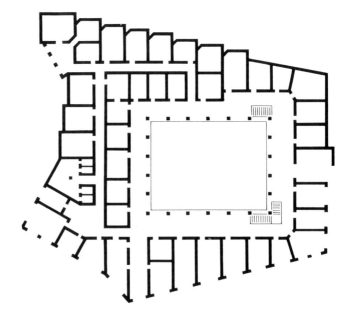

Ottoman era. They served simultaneously as a market and stock-exchange for various kinds of goods (similar to the medieval 'fondacchi' of Italy). Names like Pirintsch-Han (Rice Market) Tus-Han (Salt Market) or even Kürktschüler-Han (Furriers' Market) show that each han was the center of a certain commercial guild. Here merchants exhibited their goods and did business.

The Ottoman hans in Anatolia usually have two storeys; the lower is occupied by shops and store-rooms, and the upper by living rooms. Each room can be reached from open arcaded galleries set around a rectangular courtyard. These rooms are brightly lit and equipped with hearths and shelves. Floors are covered either with carpets or mats. Guests had to bring their own bedding. As in Anatolian houses, the upper storeys were accessible via the courtyards by means of staircases.

In the center of the courtyard was a large fountain used for washing before prayer (as in mosque courtyards). The direction of Mecca was indicated by a simple stone plaque. The large medieval hans in Anatolia had a small one-roomed mosque in the courtyard, whereas in the Ottoman period only the Ipek-Han (Silk Market) in Bursa had a small mosque in its courtyard. This is one of the city's oldest hans.

The small mosque of Ipek-Han is a two storey-ed building on an octagonal plan. The prayer room is on the upper floor. The ground floor consists of a basin with fountains on all sides. Eight massive pillars and, in between, low stone sills, surround the basin. On the exterior, the pillars are connected by pointed arches. In the center of the basin is a domed octagonal mescit. An exterior wood staircase leads to the prayer-room. The ceiling of this room is not vaulted as below, but consists of level layers of timber. A rather steep tent-like roof, like that of the

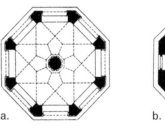 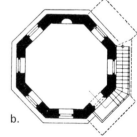

a.   b.

▲The small mosque in the courtyard of Ipek-Han in Bursa: Elevation and plans
a. Ground floor   b. Upper storey

Gihannuma tower, covers this small mosque.

The Istanbul hans are no larger, but usually have three storeys. To avoid having irregularly shaped rooms (because of the winding streets) the façade is interrupted by projections supported on consoles. An interesting façade is that of the Hasan Pasha Han in Instanbul, with its long row of triangular projections.

Plans for hans did not vary greatly from customary patterns. The courtyards were generally rectangular-shaped with external staircases on the sides. An exception is the cross-shaped staircase in the center of the Ruskon Pasha Han courtyard, its four parts leading to the galleries.

Hans, as well as Hamams, were donated by Sultans, Statesmen or wealthy citizens. The han and hamam were only unofficially part of the Külliye. There is rarely a Külliye without a hamam and han in its immediate vicinity. This dates back to the Bursa period, and was never abandoned (see the Süleyman Külliye) – indeed, donating a han was part of Oriental Islamic tradition.

Building

There are unfortunately no exact plans of large mosques which might clarify their building methods. Whether or not such plans existed at all we do not know: but certainly the architect must have presented the Sultan with some kind of plan. The few contemporary sketches that still exist are schematic sketches which were used to supplement the Sultan's building order, and lack absolute scales.

Celâl Esad noted in 'L'Art Turc' that detailed building plans rarely existed. In his opinion they were not even necessary since at the time of Hayreddin or Sinan, building had reached an unusually high standard. The quantitative designs of the arches, capitals and pillars were laid down by the master architects and were followed so fluently by the various craftsmen that only a few explanations on the part of the architect were necessary for the accomplishment of the building. Celâl Esad emphasizes that

the artistic level and the technical perfection which Ottoman architecture achieved in Sinan's time should not only be attributed to him but also to a large group of highly gifted, independently working men.

The appointment of the most outstanding artist in the country as palace architect had

▼ Example of painted tiles used in the interior decoration of Turkish Mosques

180

become customary by the beginning of the Ottoman period. Through the centuries the work of a palace architect became increasingly important. Apart from work directly connected with the palace, he had to concern himself with all building in general; and public and military works, ranging from bridges to aqueducts, were completed under his supervision.

Building Materials and Color Effects

Fine-grained gray sandstone was the basic material used in Ottoman religious building. The gray stone walls and lead-covered domes lent the Ottoman mosque a uniform color. From the very beginning the Ottomans had shown a reluctance for color and had obtained their effects by contrasting light and dark surfaces on the façades. The Yeschil mausoleum in Bursa with its tiled façades and the rich stone ornamentation on the gate of the Yeschil-Cami are last remainders of the Seljuk style.

▲ Border decorations in faience

Walls stratified with alternate stone and brick, a technique commonly used by the Byzantines, was rarely employed in Ottoman religious architecture. The mosque of Murad I in Bursa is the only example of a Sultan's mosque with colored walls. Sinan used this technique in only very few mosques built in the vicinity of the capital (the mosques of Sinan Pasha and Zal Mahmut). It occurs more often in functional buildings (baths and houses) that form part of the Külliye. While the exteriors of mosques gained their effect from their monochrome appearance, the interiors, however, were very different. Floors were colorful and carpets usually red. Walls were decorated with brilliantly painted tiles: green or blue on a white background with relatively little red. Walls without tile-decoration, together with the interior of the domes, were usually covered with paintings. Light filtering through painted glass upper-windows intensified the colors of the dome. The light and color of the interiors thus formed a great contrast with the severe exteriors.

House Construction

Timber and rough brick are the two materials usually used in construction of Turkish houses. Whereas brick, with a few exceptions, was restricted to Central Anatolia and was uniform in its method of application, timber was used variously in different regions.

Coarse brick houses with flat roofs are peculiar to Konya and its surroundings. This kind of building, since earliest times typical of the Near East and Asia Minor, can still be found in Central Anatolia today. Although not very durable, it is particularly suited to the climate of the region since it protects interiors from the extreme variations of temperature always experienced there. The flat roofs are built around an inner court, and are usually covered with a thick layer of earth, which gives protection from the extreme heat in summer.

There are three different kinds of timber construction: the dried or baked-brick framework;

external timber-covered framework; and external enamel-covered framework. Half-timbered houses of red brick are typical of Ankara, whereas wooden structures are typical of the town-dwellings and Yalis of Istanbul. Examples of the latter can be found in the Bursa region and in West Anatolia. The Bursa houses are especially attractive with their brightly decorated walls. The central and diagonal beams of the wooden structure, as well as the intervening bricks, are covered with plaster, while the corner and horizontal beams remain visible. In this way the underlying structure is clearly shown. The contrast between the darker wood areas and the gaily painted walls emphasizes the contours and the beautiful proportions of the façade.

In their religious buildings the Turks favored stone, a plain and durable material. However, they developed laws of structure of a non-tectonic nature. They gave a new meaning to the use of stone and developed it in a crystal-like formation. Yet a new interpretation in the use of building material was never sought in domestic architecture. Buildings were always developed from the nature of the materials used, and were adapted to the geographical and climatic nature of each region.

Bibliography

1. General

Akgün, A.
Landschaft und Standort als bestimmende Einflüsse auf die Gestalt der Stadt Istanbul. Arch. Diss. Zurich 1959.

Aslanapa, O.
Edirnede Osmanli Devri Abideleri, Istanbul 1949.

Diehl, Ch.
Constantinople. Paris 1924.

Diez, E.
Die Kunst der Islamischen Völker. (Encyclopaedia of the Aesthetics). Berlin-Neubabelsberg 1915.

Diez, E. and Glück, H.
Alt Konstantinopel. Munich 1920.

Diez, E. and Glück, H.
Die Kunst des Islams. Berlin 1925. (Propylaen-History of Art).

Edhem Pasa
L'Architecture Ottomane. Istanbul 1875.

Esad, C.
Constantinople, de Byzance à Stamboul. Paris 1919.

Esad, C.
L'Art Turc. Istanbul 1939.

Gabriel, A.
Monuments Turcs d'Anatolie. Paris 1931-1934.

Gabriel, A.
Voyages archéologiques dans la Turquie orientale. Paris 1940.

Gabriel, A.
Une Capitale Turque, Brousse. 2 vols. Paris 1958.

Glück, H.
Die Kunst der Osmanan. Leipzig 1922.

Gurlitt, C.
Die Baukunst Konstantinopels. 3 vols. Berlin 1912.

Hammer-Purgstall, J.v.
Auf einer Reise von Konstantinopel nach Brussa. Pesth 1818.

Hürlimann, M.
Byzanz-Konstantinopel-Istanbul. Zurich 1955.

Montani Efendi
Die Ottomanische Baukunst. Vienna 1873.

Parvillée, L.
Architecture et décoration turques. Paris 1874.

Texier, Ch.
Asie mineure. Paris 1862.

Unsal, B.
Turkish Islamic Architecture. London 1959.

Wilde, H.
Brussa. Berlin 1909.

2. Historical

Babinger, F.
Mehmet der Eroberer und seine Zeit. Munich 1953.

Danismend, I. H.
Izahlı Osmanlı tarihi Kronolojisi. Istanbul 1947-1950.

Evliya Celebi
Seyyahatname. (Translated into English by J. v. Hammer-Purgstall: Narrative of travels in Europe, Asia and Africa). London 1834-1850.

Hacı Kalfa (Kâtip Celebi)
Cihan-Numâ. Istanbul 1732-1733.

Hammer-Purgstall, J. v.
Geschichte des Osmanischen Reiches. 4 vols. Pesth 1827-1835.

Lybyer, A. H.
The Government of the Ottoman Empire in the Time of Süleyman the Magnificent. London s.d.

Mayer, L. A.
Islamic Architects and their Works. Geneva 1956.

Moltke, H. v.
Briefe aus der Türkei. Berlin 1911.

Sherrard, Ph.
Konstantinopel, Bild einer heiligen Stadt. (German translation by F. Burckhardt.) Olten, Lausanne and Freiburg i.B. 1963.

Toynbee, A. J.
Der Gang der Weltgeschichte. (German translation of D. C. Somervell's book 'A Study of History') Zurich s.d.

Unver, S.
Fatih Külliyesi ve Zamani. Istanbul 1946.

3. Mosques

Anhegger, R.
Eski Fatih Camii meselesi, in 'Tarih Dergisi,' vol. 6, 1954.

Gabriel, A.
Les Mosquées de Constantinople, in 'Syria,' 1926.

Vogt-Göknil, U.
Türkische Moscheen (French edition: Les Mosquées Turques). Zurich 1953.

4. Baths

Aru, A. K.
Türk Hamamlari. Istanbul 1949.

Glück, H.
Die Bäder Konstantinopels (Problems of Dome Building). Vienna 1921.

Klinghardt, K.
Türkische Bäder. Stuttgart 1927.

5. Sinan

Akurgal, E.
Sanattarihi bakımından Sinan, in 'Ankara Universitesi dil, tarih-cografya dergisi,' Ankara 1944.

Babinger, F.
The Turkish Renaissance. Comments on the works of the great Turkish architect Sinan in 'Beiträge zur Kenntnis des Orients,' vol. 11, 1914.

Corbett, S.
Sinan, Architect in Chief to Süleyman the Magnificent in 'The Architectural Review,' vol. 113, May 1953.

Diez, E.
The architect Sinan and his works in 'Atlantis,' April 1953.

Egli, E.
Sinan, der Baumeister osmanischer Glanzzeit. Zurich 1954.

6. Turkish Tiles

Otto-Dorn, K.
The Islamic Iznik in 'Istanbuler Forschungen,' vol. 13, 1941.

Unsal, B.
Iznik, çinici ligine dair, in 'Mesleki teknik ögretim dergisi,' 1956.

7. Domestic Architecture

Berk, C.
Konya Evleri. Istanbul 1951.

Eldem, S. H.
Türk Odası in 'Güzel Sanatlar,' booklet 4, 1944.

Eldem, S. H.
Türk evi Tipleri. Istanbul 1959.

Osman Rifat
Edirne Sarayi. Ankara 1957.

Unver, S.
Edirne'de Fatihin Cihannuma Kasri. Istanbul 1953.

Unver, S.
Amuca Hüseyin Pasa Yalisi. Istanbul 1956.

Chronological Table

Dates	Political Events of the Ottoman Empire	Dates	Buildings of the Ottoman Empire
1299	Foundation of the Ottoman Empire by Osman.		
1326	Conquest of Bursa; Bursa becomes the capital.		
1354	The Turk's first crossing into Europe (via the Dardanelles).		
		1360–1389	Murad I Mosque, Bursa.
1361	Conquest of Adrianople; 1368 Adrianople-Edirne becomes the capital.		
		1391	Beginning of Yildirim-Beyazid Külliye in Bursa.
		1394–1413	Ulu-Cami in Bursa.
1402	Battle at Ankara between Beyazid I and Timur-Lenk.		
1403	Mongol rule of Asia Minor; Beyazid I dies in Mongol imprisonment.		
1403–1413	Struggle for power between the four sons of Beyazid.		
1413	Mohamed's victory over his brothers; Reunification of the Empire under his rule.	1413–1421	Yeschil-Cami Külliye in Bursa.
		1438–1447	Uç Şerefeli Mosque, Edirne.
1451	Mohamed II's accession to the throne.		
1453	Conquest of Constantinople.		
		1471	Mohamed II Külliye, Istanbul.
1481	Death of Mohamed II.		
		1484–1488	Beyazid II Külliye, Edirne.

185

Dates	Western Dome Buildings	Dates	Western Political Activities
		1400	Medici Family at Florence.
		1415	England's victory over France (Agincourt).
1420–1434	F. Brunelleschi completes the dome at Florence.		
1429	Pazzi Chapel in Florence.		
		1431	Liberation of Orléans; Burning of Joan of Arc.
		1438	The Hapsburg dynasty gains the German Imperial crown.
		1440	Gutenberg discovers printing.
		1449	Lorenzo il Magnifico, Florence.
		1450	Francesco Sforza, Duke of Milan.
		1460	Loss of Venetian possessions in Greece.
		1460	Pope Pius II.
1470	Santa Maria della Grazie, Milan.		
		1472	Pope Sixtus IV.
		1473	Birth of Copernicus.
1480	Leonardo's improvizations on main rooms.		
1485	Madonna delle Carceri in Prato.		
		1492	Discovery of America.
		1492	Pope Alexander VI.

Dates	Political Events of the Ottoman Empire	Dates	Buildings of the Ottoman Empire
		1501–1506	Beyazid II Mosque, Istanbul.
1520	Accession of Süleyman.		
1529	First siege of Vienna.		
		1539	Sinan's appointment as palace architect.
		1543–1548	Şehzade Mosque, Istanbul.
		1550–1556	Süleyman Mosque and Külliye, Istanbul.
		1555 (?)	Mihrimah Mosque, Istanbul.
		1555–1561	Rüstem Pasha Mosque, Istanbul.
1566	Death of Süleyman I.		
		1569–1575	Selim Mosque, Edirne.
		1570–1571	Sokullu Mosque, Istanbul.
		1588	Death of Sinan.
		1609–1616	Sultan Kara-Ahmet Mosque, Istanbul.
1683	Second siege of Vienna.		
1699	The Turk's withdrawal from Hungary, Dalmatia and Croatia.		
1839	Tanzimat—the new order.		

Dates	Western Dome Buildings		Dates	Western Political Activities
1502	Tempietto of Bramante, Rome.			
			1503	Pope Julius II.
1506	Bramante's design for St. Peter.			
1508–1606	Santa Maria della Consolazione at Todi.			
			1513	Pope Leo X.
			1521	Luther's translation of the Bible.
			1524	Peasants' Revolt.
			1527	Sacco di Roma.
1547	Michelangelo's design for St. Peter.			
			1558	Elizabeth I, Queen of England.
			1618	Beginning of the Thirty Years War.
1642	Sant'Ivo at Rome.			
			1643	Louis XIV, King of France.
1667	Capella della San Sidone, Turin.			
1668	San Lorenzo, Turin.			
			1716–1718	Prince Eugen's victories over the Turks.
			1740–1780	Maria Theresa, Empress of Austria.
			1789	French Revolution.

Glossary

Caravanseray	Inn
Hamam	Bath
Han = Caravanseray	Inn, hostel
Harem	Private, and Women's Apartments
Kasir	Summer-house
Kibla	South-east wall facing Mecca.
Köschk	Garden pavilion
Külliye	Mosque with adjoining public buildings.
Medrese	Theological School
Meschid	Small Mosque
Mihrab	Praying niche
Mimber	Pulpit
Saray	Sultan's residence
Sedir	Bench
Selâmlik	Men's apartments
Sofa	Hall
Türbe	Tomb or Mausoleum
Vakf	Donation
Vakfiye	Deed of donation
Yali	Summer seaside residence

Acknowledgements

The author wishes to thank the following persons without whose invaluable help this book would not have been possible: Dr. Hayrullah Örs, Director of the Top Kapi Museum at Istanbul; Madame Seniha B. Göknil; Professor S. Ünver. The author also wishes to thank the numerous publishers who allowed material to be reproduced, in particular the following: Editions de Boccard, Paris (for the drawings by A. Gabriel, pages 48 and 49); Verlag für Architektur, Zurich (for the drawings by Le Corbusier and extracts from his 'Carnets de Voyages' in his 'Complete Works,' Vol. I, pages 4 to 8); and the Review, 'du Atlantis,' Zurich (for the drawings by Fossati, pages 94, 139, 143 and 147).

Table of Contents